C000070942

PARENT LIKE YOU
MEAN IT

PARENT LIKE YOU MEAN IT

Raising Extraordinary Children in the Age of Mediocrity

D. I. CLARK

ISBN: 978-0-578-35661-7 (hardback)

The conclusions and opinions expressed in this book are those of the author
and are based on her personal experience with her own children. They do not
inherently reflect the outcomes of other parents and no guarantees are im-
plied if you choose to implement the principles contained in this book.

First Printing, 2022

ParentLikeYouMeanIt@gmail.com

For my husband and children

Contents

Foreword

Congratulations! If you have purchased *Parent Like You Mean It: Raising Extraordinary Children in the Age of Mediocrity*, you are trying to be the best parent you can be for your child. Additionally, you may be considering the alternatives to daycare or traditional school for your small human and trying to figure out what that might look like. Spoiler Alert: It will be challenging. As a parent, you will not receive professional accolades, paid time off, promotions, or raises. You may not drive the nicest car, own the fanciest home, or post the most exotic vacation photos in your friend circle. Some days, memories of your pre-parenting life may seem like a walk in a park full of rainbows and butterflies.

As I read *Parent Like You Mean It*, I was struck by Ms. Clark's frequent references to "modeling good or desired behavior" and her kids "learning by osmosis". That only happens when you make a well-thought-out plan and then consistently follow your plan. Ms. Clark did not successfully raise her children because she had elusive magical powers reserved for select parents. She successfully raised responsible and independent young adults, because she actively invested her time and energy into teaching her children moral values and remained laser-focused on parenting her children with patience, fortitude, determination, and a strategic vision.

Contrary to what the daycare/early childhood education industry would have us believe, raising children to be decent human beings does not take a team of experts. It got complicated when two-income households became the norm and a non-family member took over supervising babies, toddlers, and pre-school age kids for ten hours a day, five days a week. Industry is created to make money, and the more bells, whistles, and shiny gadgets a childcare center has, the higher tuition will be and the better parents will feel about turning their children over to its care every morning. A real or imaginary wait list ups the ante! I'm not saying childcare centers are inherently bad, because they are not. They are an absolute necessity for single parents and in situations where both parents must work to provide for the needs (which are different than wants) of the family. However, if keeping your children home is an option, I believe it is the best choice.

Although my family and the Clark family have never met in person, we made similar choices and had comparable parenting styles. My wife had a high-risk pregnancy and we knew that having additional children wasn't an option. We had one chance to turn our bundle of joy into a decent, caring, responsible human being and, frankly, the idea of handing her over to someone else to do the majority of the work was simply terrifying. My wife put her career on hold and became a full-time mom. We were solidly middle income, but economic choices were made. We were thrifty, and became experts on free and low-cost entertainment: story time at the local library, neighborhood playgroups, state, county and city parks, and camping trips. There are still recipes for play-doh and bubbles in our recipe box and directions for making a geodesic dome out of rolled up newspaper in a file, just in case. And we managed this before the internet was widely available and the go-to source for things to do everywhere on Earth! Household rules were simple and designed to promote health and safety and prevent childish actions from torpedoing future life. For example, wear a bicycle helmet even if it's hot and gives you helmet hair, think twice about posting things on the "forever" internet, and remember nothing good happens when you are out after midnight. The natural consequences of actions will teach an incredible number of lessons if you let them!

Being the at-home parent does not necessarily fall to mom. My career took an unexpected turn when our daughter was ten and my wife and I switched roles. She resumed her career and I became the master of kid-related activities. This was a bit of a bumpy transition for everyone. I had a LOT to learn. But I believe the time I was able to spend hands-on, in the trenches, parenting every day, had a positive effect on our family and I wouldn't trade it for anything.

When your child reaches school age, there are more decisions to be made. Once upon a time, everyone went to the neighborhood pubic school and got a pretty solid education. Now, school has become politicized, teachers have a powerful union, and curriculum changes with the tides of political correctness. Private or parochial school may or may not be a better option. If you choose to homeschool, it isn't necessary to invent this particular wheel all by yourself. Homeschooling has existed as long as there have been children. Great resources abound! A quick Google search will yield a long list of private online schools, homeschool parent co-ops, tutoring centers, published curriculum, and virtual classes at every level. When your student is older, he or she can take specific classes at a local public or private school, or dual enroll at the local state college.

Allendale Academy (a private "umbrella" school for homeschool families) was privileged to work with the Clark family on their homeschool adventure. Ms. Clark was uniquely qualified to be her children's primary educator because, as their mom, she knew each child's strengths, weaknesses, and learning style, thus enabling her to choose the best curriculum to foster their success. She was also organized and detail-oriented, providing timely report cards, attendance records, and re-enrollments to Allendale. We maintained current transcripts for each of her children, provided advice on college-preparatory classes and kept track of high school graduation requirements. As an "umbrella school", Allendale also provided the recognized legal framework for the Clark's homeschool, sending official transcripts to the colleges and universities to which her children applied and providing proof of enrollment for part-time jobs, scholarships, and auto insurance.

If you haven't developed a strategic plan for your parenting, Ms. Clark's *Parent Like You Mean It* will help you do just that. With clarity, humorous anecdotes, and practical suggestions, she offers an easy-to-implement framework for parents who hope to effectively instill values into their child and raise responsible human beings. Whether you are parenting alone or with a partner, Ms. Clark's insights and ideas will provide food for thought and practical guidance. Happy reading!

Ray Collins
School Director, *Allendale Academy*

Introduction

If you are a parent, I wrote this book for you.

We all have different starting points, different children, different circumstances and different inputs that mold our lives and parenting styles. However, I believe there are straightforward parenting principles that transcend these differences and target shared concerns of caring parents.

For over fifteen years, those around me have repeatedly suggested I write a book about parenting. I do not hold focused degrees in child development, education or psychology. I have not spent years conducting empirical research in educational methodology or teaching practices. And I certainly did not approach writing this book as an expert in the field of parenting.

But maybe, that's exactly why I have been encouraged to write a book about parenting.

Who am I, then? And what makes me qualified to recommend a strategic approach to parenting?

I am a mom. I have two grown children who are successful in their lives and careers. And throughout 24 years of parenting my children (homeschooling them along the way), I have accumulated a lot of experiential and observational data. I have read voraciously; I have communicated often with other moms and dads traversing this journey we call "parenting"; and, as you will undoubtedly conclude, I have developed many opinions along the way.

I have taught children of all ages since I was fourteen years old. With my first job (in the late 1970s) I was given the daunting responsibility of teaching children ages four months to two years old to swim. I had no certified credentials except I happened to be a strong swimmer myself. I was "shown the ropes" by a veteran swim instructor ... a sixteen-year-old who trained me for a grand total of one hour before my first student—a squalling four-month-old—was unceremoniously plopped into my arms. And into the pool we went. I held that job for about two years. During that time period, not only did all of my students survive, but they also learned to swim and respect their instructor. I also learned a lot: how to focus, distract, motivate and challenge my little charges.

I have been a camp counselor, I have taught all sorts of physical activities such as cardio training, strength training, and two martial arts to children and adults of all ages; and not least, I have raised and educated two children of my own from birth to college. In forty years of interaction with children and their parents, I have concluded our overall cultural perspective on parenting has shifted from a common-sense approach to a complex, institutionalized ordeal. Rather than applying the principles of simple maturity and self-discipline, we are led to believe that parenting requires input and validation from a suite of experts eager to convince paying customers that their family requires counseling because their toddler refuses to eat carrots. Parenting culture has changed in the last forty years; children have not.

As I interact with parents and teach their children, I get the sense that many parents feel fearful and unsure about parenting. They seem to stumble through their days, bogged down in reactive parenting and overwhelming hesitancy. They tiptoe around setting firm boundaries and shrink from disciplining their children. They hold back from administering reasonable, well-thought-out consequences when negative behavior warrants them. Many parents *say* they want the best for their children but seem to misunderstand what that really means. Compounding this fear and confusion, many so-called "experts" in the lucrative industry of parenting and counseling are "fanning the flames," capitalizing on the very insecurities they claim to address. The outcome? Indecisive parents are afraid to *actively parent* their children. The result of fearful parenting? Children "run" the show. More accurately, often *no one* runs it.

But, proactive, effective parenting is not that complex.

Now, I might guess by this point, some of you are shooting flaming darts at me, and that's okay. I realize there can be complicated situations and extenuating circumstances that require specialized and long-term counseling. This book is not about those exceptions. This book is about everyday human nature and contains nuggets that parents in *any* circumstance can apply to child-raising.

What is "the Best" for Our Children?

I believe most parents really want the best for their children. I also believe *many* have a misguided understanding of what that means and how to go about parenting for those results.

What is "the best" for our children? For some parents, "the best" means somehow making things easier for their children by not allowing them to experience whatever events they remember as being painful in their own upbringing. For others, "the best" may mean allowing their children to experience financial affluency early on—advanced electronics, expensive family vacations, private schools, and the like. Some parents want to provide their children with better growth and educational experiences than they had, and this is their definition of "the best".

While some parents may have defined their own specific, customized definition of "the best" for their children, others may have not strategically considered how they define "the best" for their kids. This void creates *parenting without principle*. Absent a deliberate definition of "the best" for your children, the cultural norm will fill that vacuum. When that happens, parents can find themselves completely distracted from the real business of parenting and focusing instead on superficial sidetracks like getting their children smart phones, purchasing athletic shoes that cost $150 for the little logo on the side, or allowing Susie to attend Friday night's homecoming football game even though she has a D in math class. When that happens, common sense has flown out the window, and with it, Susie's future.

Well, then, what is "the best" for our children as a whole?

As a starting point, it is helpful to reflect on what parenting was like a generation ago. I perceive an inverse relationship between the increased amount of societal attention on making parenting a complex task requiring experts and the correlating positive outcomes for our children. A century ago, there was little to no industry built around parenting. Adults grew up, had children and spent much more energy focusing on raising them properly. Children were given real responsibilities—not contrived ones—at a much earlier age. They learned how to handle those responsibilities, sometimes by making mistakes in the process. Parents weren't perfect and children weren't perfect. Yet true respect, self-discipline and work ethic were far more commonplace than they are today.

Life and society are vastly different than they were a generation ago. In today's high-tech world, when success opportunities for young people abound, why is it that we have so many young adults who are troubled or just can't "find their way?" Simply stated, the more we have tried to "outsource" parenting, abandoning core, common-sense principles—respect, consequence, discipline—the more we have messed up our kids.

Today, what constitutes "the best" for our children?

In my experience, "the best" meant raising my children to:

- seek and embrace their moral center, whether religious or secular;
- coherently articulate their viewpoints to others in a respectful manner;
- remain open-minded, curious and respectful of others' moral

centers, and engage in discussion/debate, with an attitude of compassion and without an attitude of condemnation;

- enjoy life-long learning and challenge;
- develop strength in adversity and the desire/determination to do hard things;
- have a strong work ethic in all aspects of life and experience the sense of fulfilled exhaustion which comes as a result of hard physical and mental work;
- live daily with a sense of gratitude and appreciation;
- look for, create and experience joy in the world around them;
- self-develop their own unique abilities and potential;
- contribute creatively and productively to our society and world;
- recognize their choices and accept accountability for their actions, choices and the corresponding results—whether they are happy about them or not;
- foster an overall others-orientation;
- live a physically and mentally healthy life, incorporating work and play;
- actively stretch beyond their own comfort zone to fully embrace life and all its opportunities.

Note the following "popular" ideas did not make my list:

- blame other people for their own choices;
- resent people who were more advantaged or skilled than they were;
- engage in self-pity, thinking others "had it better" than they did;
- use the inherent "unfairness" of life as an excuse for suboptimal performance and lack of accountability;
- avoid respectful disagreement;
- focus on video games / TV;
- yearn for the latest toys / electronic gadgets;

- win at all costs;
- live by the motto, "Just do what makes you happy".

Are some successful adults the product of parents who relied heavily on the modern-day myth that "it takes a village of experts to raise a child"? Of course. I would strongly suggest that these individuals are not the norm and that they succeeded *despite* the meddling of the "expert coalition", not because of it.

"Happiness" is Not the Goal

What about "happiness"? Happiness is strangely missing from my list. Happiness is a by-product of wise parenting goals; happiness doesn't exist by itself in a vacuum. Just like our children's life paths are created, so happiness and joy are also created along the way.

And yet, if you ask most parents what they want for their children, the most common answer I've heard remains, "I just want them to be happy."

That answer, perhaps more than anything else, illustrates the root of the problem. Today, with boundless opportunities to learn, to grow, to work hard, to creatively produce, to help others, to do good in so many ways ... how have we resorted to defining the *ultimate goal* for our children—who represent the future of our society—as a fleeting *emotion* that can change depending on whether or not we've had our morning coffee?

Happiness and joy are not things that "happen" to us, nor are other people responsible for making us happy. We are responsible for cultivating positive emotions within ourselves regardless of our circumstances. Other people or events cannot control the level of happiness and joy we choose to experience in our own minds and lives. It is entirely possible to be unhappy about other people's actions or our life circumstances, and still choose to be abundantly happy, peaceful and joyful! The power to choose those attitudes is within us. If we choose not to cultivate joy and happiness from within and blame our unhappiness on other people or circumstances, then we prefer the role of victim. A victim mentality lets us *shift accountability for our own unhappiness onto others*. It enables a persistent belief that others can control our emotions. It allows us to be sad and morose without learning to manage our emotions and feelings. It allows us to justify our lack of responsibility, accountability, discipline. Choosing to dwell in unhappiness is the easy way out and is not a positive role model for our children.

Happiness is not continuous in life. We all have time periods in our lives when we feel happy, and likewise, when we are simply not happy. That is the essence of being human. Ironically, the juxtaposition of these contrasts is what allows us to recognize the emotion of happiness. Peace and happiness often develop as a result of adversity and our cumulative choices to discipline our minds and emotions.

As parents, we have the responsibility to teach our children happiness is an emotion they can cultivate even if things are not going their way. We have the privilege of helping our children learn to make their own choices, wisely and effectively. We have the responsibility to teach our children to be responsible for their own thoughts and actions. Despite the fact we all want to be happy and we want our children to be happy, happiness in itself is not a goal; it is an outcome.

I am frequently asked for parenting advice. Often this happens in context with complimenting one of my children. An open-ended question will be posed, like, "How did you do it?" Obviously, there are lots of paths successful parents may ultimately take. Like anything worthwhile, the results you get will be determined by the effort and time you invest in the process. However, there are guiding principles that can help you be the parent your child needs and deserves. If you're already in the midst of the grand adventure we call "parenting", these principles can help you adjust if needed, perhaps making the path forward less conflict-ridden for you and your child. If you don't yet have children, consider implementing these principles as a whole, realizing your parenting outcome will be optimal when you have the advantage of starting with a strong foundation.

You may find yourself agreeing with some things I say and disagreeing with other things I say. That's okay. You can choose to agree or disagree with my viewpoints. You can choose to use or not use these principles—or modify them as you see fit for your family and circumstances. In the end, the responsibility for these choices—and the resulting consequences—are yours.

Throughout this book, rather than references to "expert" scientific studies and "diagnostic" tools, expect to hear my observations on common-sense, straightforward parenting. Expect to read anecdotes from both my own experience and my years of interaction with other parents. Expect to discover parenting is a journey demanding continuous self-improvement as you strive to raise your children well. And expect to realize no matter what your situation, it is indeed possible for you to parent like you mean it.

2

Prioritize Parenting

It Takes a Lot of Time and Sacrifice

In my interactions with parents, I have observed many appear more focused on themselves than on their parenting. Competing priorities and distractions in their lives have multiplied to the point of losing sight of their overarching responsibility to parent. And while I won't argue that taking care of your own mental, physical, emotional and spiritual well-being is an important prerequisite to being a good parent, I will argue these activities need to be modified, once you choose to become a parent. It's not all about you anymore.

If you want to do your best to ace this "parenting thing", then you likely have to put some of your wants on hold for a while. Parenting is an enormous, often all-absorbing undertaking. "Parenting" is an action verb. There is no room for passivity in effective parenting. Failure to recognize, accept and embrace this fact quickly leads to parenting frustration and by correlation, ineffective parenting.

The great majority of frustrations I have heard from parents seem rooted in an unspoken cultural expectation that parenting shouldn't take so much *time*. Although they don't actually say it, some parents seem to view parenting as a hobby they do "on the side."

Understanding and embracing the sheer enormity of the time commitment you make once you become a parent is one of the most important factors in creating parenting effectiveness. Accept it—don't fight it. Parenting is *supposed* to take a lot of time. Parenting is *supposed* to take a lot of energy. Parenting produces *human beings.* Ideally, it generates human beings of good character, who are productive contributors within society. What other profession can lay claim to that? How can the raising of excellent human beings possibly be an insignificant pursuit?

Parenting requires personal sacrifice, and that does not seem to be a popular cultural concept nowadays. Instead of hearing about parental sacrifice, we hear about "Me time." We hear platitudes and slogans such as, "You have to take care of yourself and your needs first. You can't give from an empty pitcher." These sentiments did not exist forty years ago, at least in the mainstream population. The emphasis on self-focus at the expense of parenting has fundamentally missed the point of what parenting is all about. It's about your kids. It's not about you.

In my experience, children need lots of parental time. Children need lots of parental attention. Children need to know parents are consistently there, and that parents will sacrifice to take care of them. My children wanted to be near me often, whether I was folding laundry, doing the dishes, making meals, going grocery shopping or using the bathroom (I drew the line there! Even a parent needs some bathroom privacy.) Giving a child lots of parental time doesn't translate into an unnatural scenario where an overabundance of unnecessary attention is riveted on the child for no apparent reason other than to indulge his every whim. The discerning parent studies his child and does a constant balancing act of providing the right amount of attention at the right time.

I have heard parents object to putting their personal goals on hold, lamenting missed opportunities that may not come again in the same form. Ironically, they fail to recognize that putting their *parenting* on hold might have a more disastrous impact on their future lives, their child's life and society as a whole, than putting their own desires on hold. Each day of your child's life carries with it an opportunity cost that cannot be redeemed at a future date. Each day of your parenting adventure carries with it an opportunity cost that cannot be discounted. You can't hit a "pause" button and put the raising of your child on hold, to be resumed when it is more convenient for you. Your child will grow up quickly, whether or not you choose to make time for him or her. There are no rewinds in your child's life. Once childhood is gone, it is gone forever. You cannot get back the days you missed.

Whether or not you have accomplished what you wanted to accomplish prior to becoming a parent is irrelevant in determining the best way to parent your child *after* you become a parent. Likewise, whether or not you had a normal or dysfunctional childhood should not be a consideration in deciding whether or not you are going to do *your* best to create a positive situation for your child. As the adult, you have to figure out how to get *your* act together so you can parent enthusiastically and energetically. That is your duty and obligation.

Quality Time Does Not Equal Quantity Time

Children require *quantity* time, not just a quick, hurried hour in the morning and another hour in the evening, if they are to grow, thrive and become well-adjusted adults. The idea that quality time can be dispensed in doses like a drug and have the same results as maximal *immersion* in quality time defies logic. Think of learning a foreign language. If you study a little here and there, you may eventually pick up the basics of a language. But language immersion is one of the best ways to actually learn the language, with all its nuances and vernacular permutations. The language of parenting is no different. In order to observe and learn how to best parent your child, you need to be immersed as much as possible in the business of parenting. In order for your child to observe and learn how to respond to the instruction of a firm yet loving parent, he needs to be immersed in the job of childhood.

The synergy between quality and quantity time is critically important, because I think children derive their sense of security, in part, not
from seeing a parent in sporadic, bite-sized chunks of time, but from
seeing a parent is *there* and *present*. Whether dad is making breakfast on
a weekend morning, or mom is folding laundry at the end of the day
does not really matter to a child. Too many parents worry about continuously entertaining their children. It is wonderful to make time to
play with your child if you can. But he can be trained to entertain himself. Maximum parental presence and devotion are key inputs in your
child's growth process. Parental presence creates consistency, stability
and reliability in his emotional, chaotic world. I believe it is a major
contributing factor in a child's healthy development of self-confidence.
"Presence" here does not just mean a warm body sitting nearby. Authentic "presence" expresses itself in a parent who is able, willing and
desirous of engaging with his child while simultaneously folding the
laundry, preparing meals, putting groceries away, exploring outside or
constructing magnificent block creations together. Authentic presence
is not overly indulgent. It expresses itself as genuine interest in the little
human beings who have been brought into a family.

How is a parent's authentic presence critical to the development of
a child's sense of security and confidence? It is critical, because a child
benefits from having a unified, consistent set of behavioral boundaries
to follow. When a child knows the rules, he understands where the lines
are between what he can do and what he is not permitted to do.

The child whose attends daycare, school and perhaps aftercare has
multiple sets of behavioral boundaries he is expected to somehow learn
and navigate when he doesn't even know how to control *himself* yet.
Having no idea of what constitutes good or proper behavior, he is
thrown into a gumbo soup of do's and don'ts and is supposed to somehow figure out what is acceptable and what is not. Children seem to
be subconsciously desperate to know where their behavioral boundaries
lie. When the boundaries aren't consistent and clear, the only way for
them to figure out what the limits are is to continually test *all* of the
boundaries.

If your child experiences multiple boundaries on a regular basis because he does not have a stay-at-home parent, it is especially critical for you to make the most of the hours spent with your child. With precious limited time together, it might be tempting to "let him get away" with less than desirable behaviors; after all, enforcing consequences for misbehavior is not nearly as "fun" as playing games together! It also might be tempting to plop your child or yourself down in front of the TV instead of engaging with each other, because you are tired after a long work day. However, if you are in a situation where your child bounces between boundary sets during his day, I believe it is vital to commit to enforcing your family boundaries consistently and predictably *whenever* you are with him. That way, you help lessen his confusion about appropriate conduct.

Parenting proactively by establishing your family values and principles positions you to be more effective than parenting from a reactive stance. These principles can serve as guideposts for your child, directing him towards the morals and norms you wish to instill. Reactive parenting waits for misbehavior to occur and then responds to it. Proactive parenting anticipates when and how misbehavior is likely to occur and attempts to minimize the potential for it. In my experience, proactive parenting creates more positive attitudes in both parents and children.

If you are a stay-at-home parent, you have the opportunity to create one set of consistent norms—principles based on your chosen moral center—and lovingly, yet firmly enforce those principles throughout the entire day. When behavioral and moral principles are taught to a child beginning at a young age, the child has an opportunity to naturally internalize what he should do and how he should act, not only at home, but in many situations. He learns not only from direct parental teaching, but also by example and osmosis. Simply by observing family principles in action all day long, he can absorb many lessons about behavior, speech and life. Because there is one set of boundaries, he is not confused. Because the enforcement of those boundaries by a parent is consistent, your child does not have to worry about who is in control. He can then set about his real business of being a child.

Testing the Waters

Now, as many parents will attest, children *will always* test boundaries. You, as the parent, are responsible for making boundaries clear and easy to understand. When small children bear the burden of trying to shift from one set of boundaries to another multiple times a day, they remain in a continual state of flux—they do not know or understand the rules or why they keep changing. I believe this uncertainty makes it much harder for them to develop an innate sense of security.

Our young son had a particular penchant for boundary testing from the time he first emerged from the womb. When he was eighteen months old, we moved to a new house. As we settled into our new home, I began mopping the floors. Because they were tile, I was concerned about our little tyke slipping and falling while the floors were still wet. It was clear to me at this age he knew and understood when I told him not to come onto the floor, so I allowed him to play nearby. He was extremely interested in watching me use the mop (Household, kitchen and functional items are always so much more interesting to children than regular toys!) As he inched closer, I reminded him patiently and repeatedly not to step on the tile floor, because it was wet and he could fall. I also told him if he did not obey me, he would go to his room until the floors were dry. This was not an emotional or dramatic interchange. I simply used words he could understand to explain the boundary (quite literally, where the carpet met the tile), the behavioral expectation, the basic reason (it is not always necessary to explain your reasons, but in this situation, it was appropriate), and the consequence if he disobeyed.

His impish grin grew larger as he continued to shuffle toward the wet floor. The look on his face screamed, "Do you dare me?" I repeated myself a few times (children need repetition, and a lot of it!) and continued mopping. A moment later, when I looked up to check on him, I saw one pink, plump big toe squirm onto the soaking wet floor.

Simultaneously, he looked up at me. The challenge on his face was clear. Was I really going to do anything about it or not? Was the boundary real or pretend? Was I going to parent or not? Was I in control—or was he?

I calmly put down the mop, swooped him into my arms and carried him off to his room. I put the gate up at his door and told him I would get him out when I was done mopping and the floors were dry. He was not happy! The inevitable wailing and screaming ensued. I made sure he had several books and toys to play with and calmly went about my mopping. Within minutes, he had successfully distracted himself with a story book. He had tested the waters and found out I meant what I said. It is micro-moments like these—hundreds of them each week in the life of your small child—where the battle for his obedience and future respect is either won or lost.

Navigating these moments successfully takes time, as well as physical and mental stamina. It takes parental focus, a strategic mindset and tactics that support your overall parenting goals. It takes a caring parent who is willing to be present as much as possible in his child's life. Quality and quantity time is a gift you give your child that will be paid back in spades as he grows into a secure, productive and responsible citizen.

People curiously ask me, "What's the greatest gift you have given your children?" My answer is time. Long, long stretches of time—to play outside, to feel the wind on their faces, to spin around in the breeze, to look at the sky. My time as well, long stretches of silent and comforting companionship with them, books read aloud, times of correction, education, play, conversation, laughter, debate and discovery.

If you spend lots of time with your child when he is young, doing old-fashioned fun things together, you help to build the pipeline for open communication when he is older. Special, critical teenage conversations can't happen during small slices of time, and they certainly can't be scheduled. Those discussions also won't happen if you haven't spent time in his younger years building trust.

The likelihood of your teenager talking to you about lots of *stuff* increases if you have been there listening from the beginning. The most meaningful conversations I had with my teenagers happened unexpectedly, often in the wee hours of the morning when we both were exhausted. You can't force your child's heart to open up to you. You have to be there when he wants to talk. That takes time.

The gifts of parental quality and quantity time are gifts of sacrifice. They can't be replaced by expensive family vacations or trips to huge theme parks. These types of extravagances may create wonderful memories, but you can create equally amazing memories without spending a dime. Your reliable presence and enthusiasm in helping your child to discover the wonders of the natural world all around him are all that is necessary.

Do not expect your child to recognize or appreciate the gift of time you freely give him. That is not his role, nor is it a realistic expectation of him. As a child, he is not capable of understanding parental sacrifice. He does not have the perspective, life experience or thinking patterns of an adult. You brought him into this world. It is your responsibility to give him your time. It is your child's role to be a child. When your child is an adult, he will likely thank you for giving him your time. He will meet peers who have not had the benefit of parental devotion. He will begin connecting the dots and considering how your efforts contributed to his success. But don't expect thanks before he is...about thirty years old or so. If it happens earlier, consider yourself very fortunate!

There are No Rewinds

Creating a child-centered home full of selfish little cretins is not the goal. The goal is effective, successful parenting. Raising your child to be a wonderful, productive person in this world— succeeding in his potential and sharing his unique gifts to make this world a better place—is more important than what you might want personally from moment to moment. Raising your child is a time-urgent task, because each and every day in your child's life counts. Once each day is over, it is over—gone, gone, gone forever. You cannot recreate it.

And if you feel like parenting may involve too much sacrifice, or you simply don't wish to invest the time and energy it takes to *really* parent, then I would suggest using highly reliable birth control and consider getting a low-maintenance pet—instead of producing human beings who inherently are high-maintenance creatures from birth through adulthood.

3

Determine Your Destination

What Will You Consider "Parenting Success?"

When your child is "all grown up," what kind of person do you want her to be? What character traits and morals do you plan to instill in her to achieve that? Before you had children, did you spend time thinking about your overall goals and philosophy of parenting? I imagine some have done that, while others may be scratching their heads and saying, "Hmmm, can't say I gave it a lot of thought."

A broad parenting philosophy gives you a strategic starting point. From there, you can develop a flexible, tactical parenting game plan—the actual *actions* of how you intend to parent.

Because taking care of a little human being is rather involved, a new parent can find herself bogged down in nitty-gritty tactics—how to feed her baby, how to get her baby to sleep, how to make sure her baby is reaching developmental milestones and how to get her baby to stop screaming or fussing fifteen—or five hundred—times a day. But tactics that address all these "how" questions are most effectively determined after you have first decided on your high-level parenting strategy.

An overall parenting strategy keeps you focused on your long-term parenting goals, and points you toward creative tactics to use at each stage of your child's development. It serves as a reliable roadmap that you come back to when you are unsure of what to do in a particular situation. Revisiting your philosophical roadmap and broad parenting goals frequently keeps you in a strategic frame of mind as you parent day by day. And as your child grows, your strategy and tactics change, grow and develop in tandem.

It is ironic to think we might spend more time planning our next vacation than we do strategizing on parenting. Most people would not dream of spending a good chunk of change on a vacation and "winging it." They spend gobs of time dreaming, deciding, planning and considering every aspect of their upcoming holiday, to ensure that all goes well and that the outcome is not only what they hope for, but also a fantastic journey. Likewise, the raising of human beings—the nurture and care of tiny, amazing, one-of-a-kind individuals who may indeed have the capacity to discover cures for now-terminal illnesses and the ability to quite literally, launch civilization into new frontiers of space exploration—should be approached and planned with thoughtful deliberation and strategic focus.

If you determine your foundational parenting strategy before you become a parent or when your child is very young, your parenting journey will be much more enjoyable.

Of course, you may prefer an impromptu venture and react as you go along. In the case of a vacation, spontaneity can be a grand adventure! In the case of parenting, it can be a nightmare.

What if you haven't determined a parenting philosophy and are already a parent? If you find yourself in reactive mode, putting out parenting fires as multiple crises arise with your child each day, it might be helpful to step back and ask yourself if you are parenting tactically or strategically.

As a strategic parent, you operate from a position of strength, knowing the core values you want to instill in your child. You calmly persevere and use creative tactics to achieve those goals, remembering that the results of your efforts won't be evident in your child's life for many years. If you parent with tactics but no overarching strategy, you may feel like you are flailing around in the dark, not knowing which challenge to address first.

Don't worry. It's not hopeless. If you recognize you are reacting to whatever your child throws your way instead of responding in a way that matches your core values, you can begin transitioning from reactive mode to responsive, *parent-directed parenting.*

Becoming a strategic parent starts with firmly grasping the character traits and values that are most important to your family. From that vantage point, you can identify your character goals and objectives for your child. In turn, this keeps you focused on implementing tactics that support and enhance your values. Alignment of your family values, goals for your child and parenting actions leads to much greater clarity—and calmness—in handling those inevitable, everyday crises.

Frame Your Parenting Strategy

How do you determine your parenting strategy and goals?

Here are some questions to get you started. Try to answer them with an open mind and without preconceived notions. You don't have to be long-winded or fancy. Your answers can be simple, straightforward and jotted down on a file card. In fact, the more succinctly you state your answers, the easier it will be to figure out what is most important to your family.

- Without limitations on what you think is possible, imagine your child as a full-fledged adult. In your best-case scenario, how would you describe her character? What kind of person do you hope she will become?
- What are your most important personal and family moral values? Try to pick no more than ten. Prioritize them in rank order.
- What values do you hope to successfully impart to your child? What characteristics *don't* you want her to have?
- How do you want her to treat and interact with other people—those she knows and those she doesn't know?

- How do you envision your relationship with your adult child?
- What kind of education do you want to provide your child?
- Consider *your* strengths and weaknesses. What do you need to change within yourself to become the best parent you can be for your children? Set three personal improvement goals with target achievement dates for yourself. After you have achieved (or made significant progress towards) those, set three more goals. Repeat.

Character Report Cards

After you have framed your parenting goals and determined your most important family values, consider developing character "report cards." Whether your children are in public, charter, private or home-school, you can use a simple grading system to create a quarterly character report card.

Character education was weighted more heavily in our home than academic education. While our academic curricula were rigorous and college-preparatory, we emphasized the importance of character grades in determining "who you are as a person, and who you want to become." I graded my children on the values that were most important to our family. We had one set of character attributes for grades three through five, a modified set for grades six through eight, and a more mature set of character attributes for grades nine through twelve.

Ongoing by nature, these attributes represent a work in progress that begins in childhood and continues throughout life into adulthood. That is why a good chunk of the attributes that are listed for grades three through five also appear on the middle and high school lists.

As a starting point, I offer the below example of the character attributes for which my children received report card grades.

Grades Three-Five

- Compassionate & Loving
- Content, Thankful & Joyful

Grades Three-Five (continued)

- Obedient & Cooperative
- Just & Merciful
- Generous & Kind
- Diligent
- Good Listener
- Self-controlled & Patient
- Respectful
- Truthful

For the middle school years, graded character attributes included all of the above (for grades three-five), with three changes: Self-controlled and Patient were broken out into separate categories and Discernment/Common Sense was added to the list.

Grades Six-Eight—Modifications

- All attributes from Grades Three to Five
- Discernment/Common Sense

For the high school years, I added categories related to work ethic and re-arranged the sequencing of lifetime character attributes that remained from the elementary and middle school years.

Grades Nine-Twelve

- Work Ethic (Diligence/Discipline/Time Management) – Overall
- in Academics
- in Family Responsibilities
- in Sports
- in Work
- in Future Goals
- Content, Thankful & Joyful

Grades Nine-Twelve (continued)

- Self-controlled & Patient
- Respectful
- Good Listener
- Truthful
- Discernment/Common Sense
- Cooperative
- Just & Merciful
- Generous & Kind
- Compassionate & Loving

When I reviewed character report card grades with my young children, I explained in simple terms what each of these attributes meant. I also consistently emphasized that character and values improvement were lifelong, ongoing processes, even for full-grown adults. I did not pressure or expect my children to be perfect in these attributes; no human beings are! What I aimed for was a slow, steady progression toward understanding the importance of and embracing these values.

Not only did I reinforce these goals at report-card time, but also throughout each and every week. Character acquisition is not a mountain that is scaled in Herculean leaps and bounds. It is conquered by baby steps and motivated persistence. It is learned through osmosis, daily micro-decisions and continual reinforcement, as you help your children discover how values can be applied in their real lives.

4

Own Your Choices

Abundance or Scarcity – Which Mindset Will You Choose?

Stepping back from parenting for a moment, examine the concept of personal responsibility.

As adults, we are responsible for the outcomes of our choices. Life is inherently unfair. We are not equivalent from birth. We have different weaknesses, strengths and upbringings. Yet, at some point in the transition to adulthood, we all possess the ability to step back and perform an honest assessment of our current situation and where we would like to head in the future. The gap between the two of those may be wider for some than for others. Some adults might have to work harder to accomplish their goals than others. But in the end, it is each individual's choice to pursue excellence, muddle through mediocrity or simply give up. If we choose to let others, our past, or our current situation stifle our work ethic, perseverance, positive attitude, and motivation to push forward, then that is also our choice. And we need to own that choice, especially when we become parents.

We can choose to view our lives with abundance or scarcity. Scarcity bemoans one's own circumstances and envies others' situations. Scarcity diminishes others' hard work and lifelong pattern of choices by saying they are "lucky". By contrast, abundance focuses on one's current situation and the potential for improvement, whether it be incremental or exponential. Abundance chooses to be happy for others' accomplishments and uses examples of excellence to motivate future achievement. It is a mindset that is generous in positivity towards other people.

It is possible to have an abundance mindset even in the midst of actual scarcity. While it may be very difficult, the choice to cultivate an abundance or a scarcity mindset is ultimately related to *attitude control*. The irony is that those who choose to cultivate an abundance mindset and focus on achieving future goals, despite finding themselves in scarce current situations, can successfully forge a positive path for themselves.

Our attitudes toward life circumstances color our approach to parenting. Attitudes play a pivotal role in determining outcomes. Parent from a place of abundance, being thankful for the young life you have been given the privilege to shape. Don't begrudge that good parenting for great results takes gobs of time and requires great sacrifice. Parenting from abundance and embracing the responsibility you bear as a parent is the opposite of parenting from scarcity and resenting your responsibilities. "Abundance parenting" produces better results for both you and your child.

Life is More About Choices than Luck

What about "luck?" How you define luck—whether it is being blessed, the work of fate or simply random chance, you are indeed "lucky" if you were born in the United States. If you were born into a loving family, you are also "lucky". But quite early in life, luck falls away, and we are left with big, small and medium-sized choices that shape the fabric of our lives.

For all of us lucky enough to inhabit planet earth, life is a constant domino game, where circumstances and decisions are the individual dominoes that make us either stand or fall. We have the power to make many decisions that affect our lives every day. If there is something you don't like, you can *choose* to change it. It might seem impossible, or you may have to work very hard to make changes, while someone else may *not* have to work very hard to accomplish the same thing. Another person may work equally hard and not achieve the same success you do. "Life" itself is indeed an inequivalent experience.

Demonstrating a strong work ethic throughout one's teenage and adult life is an individual choice. Demonstrating the willingness to sacrifice short-term gratification in favor of long-term goals is also a personal choice. Accepting accountability for your past, present and future choices is critically important as you train your child to become accountable for himself.

Stop Comparing and Start Succeeding

In terms of education, each parent needs to decide which model works best for his child and family situation. Whether his schooling decision is public, private, charter, online or homeschool, the choice is ultimately a personal one that factors in many variables, including family dynamics. No matter which option you choose, realize that your child is counting on your commitment to actively and responsibly parent him. His future depends on it.

Once you have made your schooling decision, own that choice and resolve that you will do everything possible to ensure your child receives the best education you can provide via that model. Don't look around at other parents who have chosen a different path and complain about your situation. Don't begrudge families who have more advantageous financial circumstances and claim that it is "unfair" that you are not in the same boat. Likewise, do not judge a parent who is in a difficult financial situation that you have not experienced for making decisions that you don't agree with.

A strong parenting mindset starts with the recognition that where each of us is today is tied to past decisions. Your child will absorb attitudes regarding personal accountability in part by osmosis, as he lives with you and observes the extent to which you embrace personal responsibility for your choices. Accept where you are now and start from there. Stop comparing yourself to others and be determined to succeed going forward. Your child's future success is at stake.

Envying or negatively judging another parent for having more—or fewer—decision-making options than you do is energy-sapping and counterproductive. Funnel that energy into parenting your child, not judging other parents. These contrasting perspectives also assume that you understand other parents' "background stories." In reality, few of us know the nitty-gritty details of other individuals' life paths.

For example, it is unfortunate that parents who have made the decision to homeschool often hear from others, "you're so lucky that you can homeschool your children."

Having the *option* of homeschooling as a viable educational choice for one's child can actually be the cumulative effect resulting from many decisions made in an adult's life before marrying or having children, instead of mere "luck". The decisions made as far back as our teenage years can ripple waves that impact our future options.

An illustration may provide further clarification through taking a candid look at the lives and decisions of the "Smith" family.

The Smith family's decision to homeschool and the financial ability to do so was the eventual result of choices Mr. and Mrs. Smith made individually before they even met, compounded with the decisions they made from the time they met, through the next thirteen years before having their first child.

For many years before they met, Mr. and Mrs. Smith independently chose to work hard in high school, prioritizing academics over extracurricular and leisure activities. Both of them competed in sports, participated in school clubs and worked at paying jobs. They didn't spend hours on video games, didn't participate in social media, and didn't watch a lot of television.

Mr. and Mrs. Smith both chose to apply to college and both were accepted, because their high school performance and credentials were strong and varied...a direct result of their hard work and commitment to academics in high school. In order to afford college, both of them needed to work every summer during high school and college. They took whatever summer jobs they could find and saved their earnings for college. They also chose to assume student loan debt so that their college education would not be delayed. They realized this meant they needed to work even harder in college than they had in high school, if they hoped to secure good jobs that would allow them to pay off their student loans and also support themselves after graduating.

They met during the summer after Mr. Smith's sophomore year of college and Mrs. Smith's freshman year of college. They knew early on they desired a future together. They chose to get engaged after Mrs. Smith's sophomore year of college and married after Mrs. Smith's junior year of college. By then, Mr. Smith had graduated and received multiple job offers.

After getting married, Mr. and Mrs. Smith chose to move where Mr. Smith's most promising career opportunity arose. This meant leaving family and moving far away. Mrs. Smith chose to work full time and go to school part time to finish her bachelor's degree. They agreed to live frugally and did not spend beyond their means, because they wanted to purchase a home as soon as possible. They created a spending budget and disciplined themselves to adhere to a retirement savings plan.

After Mrs. Smith graduated, she began to work full time. Together, Mr. and Mrs. Smith decided to wait a while before having children. They wanted to build their savings, so that when they did have children, they would be able to independently meet the financial needs of their family and enable Mrs. Smith to stay home and raise their children.

When they finally did have children, about twelve years after getting married, Mrs. Smith chose to leave the workplace—a choice that was made possible because of purposeful, previous choices to live off of one income, pour as much as possible into savings and never incur interest payments on credit cards.

Therefore, when Mrs. Smith chose to give up her career to stay home and raise their children, she exercised an option that she and Mr. Smith had planned for via their life, education, work and personal choices for the past seventeen years. There is a world of difference between that and "luck." Mr. and Mrs. Smith were not "lucky," but thoughtful in their choices throughout their lives. Those choices eventually led to their outcomes.

Human existence dictates that some people face more difficult life circumstances than others. Ironically, what one individual views as a hardship, another individual may view as a motivating challenge to overcome. Accepting personal responsibility means accepting responsibility for the outcomes of our choices whether they turn out good or bad, whether they make us happy or unhappy and whether we wish they were different or not. Playing the luck card, especially when seeing how others' decisions impact their lives in a different way than one's own decisions do, can make individuals feel less accountable for their own decisions. It can comfort them to think that they are where they are in their lives because of *some other reason* than the choices they have made. This is the antithesis of owning our choices.

It is not necessarily comfortable to trace one's current life situation back step-by-step, examining each significant decision made since the teen years and connecting correlating outcomes. Our culture has a strong, pervasive bias for giving teens and young adults a "pass" on accountability for their choices. But that does not change the fact that we are, in part, the by-product of our own decisions. We can rail against that idea; we can complain that the circumstances some people are born into are harder than those of others; we can lash out and blame those that have made wiser decisions than us, claiming *they* are somehow at fault for *our* own undesirable situation. But in the end, we should not underestimate the power of personal responsibility and accountability. As human beings, we have the ability to choose wisely or poorly as we make a multitude of decisions every day. The accumulation of those seemingly innocuous daily decisions is what molds and shapes our lives. And the decisions you make and attitudes you bring to your parenting will mold and shape the life of your child.

Being A Parent Is Not the Same as Becoming a Parent

With current cultural resistance to the notion of personal account-ability, how do you teach your child not only to own his choices, but also to *want* to own his choices? Begin with owning the choices you make as an adult, starting with your decision to *be* a parent. *Becoming* a parent is not the same as *being* a parent. Anyone can become a parent. But not everyone who becomes a parent actually chooses to *be* a parent.

The decision to become a parent should not be solely emotional, based on how many babies you *feel* like having. If you choose to bring another life into this world, make sure you consider and plan how you are going to care for, feed, educate and provide a strong foundation for this little person. In terms of time, finances, sacrifice, and energy…how many children can you afford?

I might want eight puppies. But if I don't have the resources to give each of those puppies the food, the veterinary care, the attention and the training they need to become well-behaved puppies instead of neighborhood terrors, then I shouldn't bring home eight puppies no matter how badly I want them. If I do so anyway, knowing I can't take care of them all properly, I am not thinking about the puppies' well-being. I am thinking of my own wants, regardless of the possible negative impacts on the puppies' lives and on the lives of other human beings with whom they interact.

On the other hand, if I think I can handle eight puppies and provide adequately for all of their needs (for at least eighteen to twenty-two years each), then getting eight puppies is perfectly okay. I can even get fifteen puppies if I am adequately prepared to give them all appropriate care and attention!

Raising children is a higher stakes endeavor than raising puppies. A thoughtful, responsible choice regarding family size is based on what is best for all immediate family members, most importantly, the children you have already brought into your family. Consider all the variables related to how well-prepared you are to *be* a parent to "x" number of children, not just *become* a parent of "x" number of children. A realistic personal assessment of your time, energy, obligations and resources will guide you toward the most responsible choice.

5

Parenting is a Profession

Degrading Expectations

In my lifetime, there has been a fundamental shift not only in the way society views children, but also in the way society downgrades parental responsibility in raising them. Not so very long ago, children used to be viewed as valuable contributors to the family unit. They were given age-appropriate responsibilities based on their strengths and weaknesses and were encouraged to have a healthy view of work. It was "expected" that teenagers would work during their high school years. Most of my high school friends managed to balance academics, extracurricular/sporting activities, and part-time jobs, in addition to chores at home. Somehow, they were able to juggle all of these responsibilities and still enjoy leisure time.

Have high school students today become suddenly inept at multitasking? Has the collective body of American teenagers morphed into a sea of gross incompetents, requiring adult intervention and protection at every turn? Parents voice concerns about why Johnny or Susie "can't handle" school and work at the same time. If this is truly the case—the majority of teenagers today cannot be successful at two important endeavors at the same time—then we are essentially claiming the current generation of teens is either genetically deficient or the generation of parents who raised them possessed low expectations for their children and successfully inculcated those diminished expectations into the psyche of their children.

Today's teenagers are equally capable of high productivity and outstanding performance levels. The extent to which a responsible parent is directly involved in actively raising her child affects how motivated and determined that child is to challenge herself, set goals for her own future and energetically work towards achieving those goals.

Humans require an incredibly long timeframe to reach adulthood, but they develop the ability to contribute progressively. Today, parents seem to consistently expect less from their children than parents of previous generations. They hover nearby, ready to whisk in at a moment's notice to save their offspring from normal, daily stresses. The "helicopter" parent prevents her child from taking on age-appropriate responsibilities, depriving her of the chance to grapple with inevitable life conflicts.

The result for children? Unforeseen levels of overprotective parenting preclude many children from gaining experiences, learning to figure things out and successfully growing through failure. The result for parents? Fear of their children's potential failure paralyzes their efforts to proactively parent.

However, failure is often the genesis for developing creative problem solving, perseverance, determination and confidence in one's abilities. Without learning to fail and overcome circumstances, individuals fail to thrive in their physical, mental, emotional and spiritual development. Ironically, being protected from normal failure throughout childhood and the teen years can result in young adults' failure to understand what it means to actually *be an adult* in our world, with all of the responsibilities, privileges, challenges—and failures—that come with it. The very nature of adulthood means that you *will* experience failure in some way.

Allowing your child to fail at times provides her with opportunity for growth and helps her internalize a process for overcoming adversity. We tend to learn, grow and remember best when we experience the natural consequences of our failures firsthand. In a very real sense, when you prevent your child from *failing at everything*, you are setting her up for a lifetime of *frustration in everything*. Without the growth experiences that inherently accompany failure, she will not have the chance to develop resilience, problem-solving and the ability to learn from her mistakes. When confronted with a potential challenge, she will lack perseverance and persistence, because she will have been trained to expect you to come whooshing in to rescue her, saving her from difficulty or hardship.

A child who has not developed the intrinsic ability to deal with failure, bounce back from it, and continue to motivate herself to persevere—without needing external reinforcement—grows into a needy young adult who lacks perspective and overreacts to normal failures as if the world is ending. The smallest setbacks can become insurmountable in her mind, wreaking havoc with her mental state. Not having the latest model of cell phone or having to miss a special event with friends in order to study for an important academic exam are seen as "hardships," because she was not given the opportunity to experience *real* challenges as she was growing up.

Don't Kennel your Kids

Financial or life circumstances arguably present difficult challenges for many parents who don't want to put their child in day care but feel they have no other option. If you find yourself in this situation, my best advice is to creatively brainstorm *all possible options* that minimize the time your child is in the care of strangers and maximize the time your child is in your care, or that of another responsible parent, caring family member or trustworthy friend.

Additionally, a close examination of your finances and budget may provide some alternative options you may not have initially considered. Is it possible to make family sacrifices by foregoing vacations, new cars, updated cell phones, restaurant visits or other *non-essential* expenses? Only you can determine what is actually feasible in your particular family dynamics. If your conclusion is that you *must* put your child in a day care setting, then your parenting perspective shifts from creating an ideal situation for your child, to maximizing time with your child in a non-ideal circumstance. You can still strive to be a great parent while you *are* with your child. But it is also realistic to expect unique challenges with a child who has multiple caregivers and differing boundary rules on a daily basis.

If you think it *might* be possible to create a parent-at-home environment (even if on a part-time basis) for your child, do not underestimate the value of prioritizing your child's upbringing and well-being over vacations, cell phones and material possessions. Sometime both parents work because they say they aspire to give their children an easier life, one with more financial luxuries. But financial luxuries are not important to raising an extraordinary child. What is most important is mom or dad *being there*, cheerfully giving the gift of their time, day in and day out, lovingly engaging with their child and simultaneously doing the repetitive, mundane tasks that are required to build a happy home.

If you conclude that it *is* financially possible to have a parent at home with your child on a full-time basis, make the priority call to put your child's upbringing over career or personal goals. The presence of a full-time parent in the home can have a reverberating effect that enhances children's daily lives and benefits the whole family.

Some career schedules lend themselves to the possibility of full-time employment *and* full-time parenting. For example, remote jobs open this option for many parents. Likewise, parents may aim for shift work schedules, which allow one parent to be working at a time, while the other parent is hands-on with the children. Inherent in these variable schedules are challenges related to parents' ability to get enough sleep to perform both roles in top form. Depending on the individuals involved and their energy levels, this can be possible. Just remember you are not a robot; you are a human being, who requires adequate rest in order to perform well in your roles. Usually, when a parent is overly stressed and under-rested, her child or spouse bears the brunt of her exhaustion.

Like most worthwhile pursuits in life, there are no guarantees that everything will be smooth sailing or turn out perfectly. The parent whose primary role is the caretaking of children and the home must view her work as a profession, have a positive attitude and roll with the invariably random nature of childrearing. No two days are the same!

Because a family is also an economic unit, this means the ideal scenario is for the other parent to provide monetary income for the family. Who takes what role and how work roles are best divided are unique family decisions. It may be that the full-time parent at home can work remotely and can contribute to the family income. It may be that the full-time provider can work remotely or in shift work and contribute to the parenting role in a significant way. Or it may be that one parent finds themselves parenting *and* providing alone. In that case, her priority should be on pursuing employment that maximizes both her time spent with children at home and the financial security of her family. Most importantly, it bears repeating that no one ever said parenting would be easy. Taking care of a puppy is easy. Taking care of a kitten is easy. Taking care of a human being is *not* always easy.

Do You Want to "Have" Children or "Raise" Children?

Many adults in our society seem to procreate because they want to "have" children, but they don't truly want to *raise* them. They want to "kind of" be parents, according to a schedule that maximizes their desires and convenience. In other words, they want to fit a child in around their already existing life and commitments, without making significant changes or giving up personally important pursuits.

Raising a child is not a task that is best approached in this type of compartmentalized fashion. A child's well-being can't be apportioned to a specific timeframe during the day. A child's needs can't be completely prescheduled or anticipated. Because parenting's "product" is ultimately a human being, it should be expected that uncertainty, randomness and large quantities of time are inherent in the "production process." If you decide to become a parent, expect it to be challenging and fraught with uncertainty at times. Likewise, if you go "all in" as a parent, you can also anticipate overwhelming joy and the reward of seeing your child grow to reach her potential. These two sides of the parenting coin—challenging uncertainty and abundant joy—can't be separated. They are inextricably welded together. And you may often find that each day is a "toss of the coin!"

6

⚜

Don't Be an Emotional Wimp

Reduce the Drama by Being Principled

We've all seen the drama played out in grocery stores and toy stores. Little Johnny wants the toy on display, and Mom or Dad says "no." Instead of deciding that the answer really *is* no, Mom or Dad is lassoed into a debate with Little Johnny, who knows how to twirl his parents around his pint-sized finger quite well...they have taught him that. Instead of staying composed and recognizing the situation for what it is—a child simply wanting his own way—Mom or Dad is roped into an emotional battle. Their communication degenerates into whining back at Little Johnny, trying to explain why he can't have the toy. Sometimes it is appropriate to explain reasons to your child; other times, it's more appropriate to say a simple, firm "no." Saying "no" to your child is not an emotional experience. It's a logical, binary, common sense exercise. Do you want to buy the toy for Little Johnny or not? If so, by all means, go ahead. If not, for *whatever* reason, make your answer, "no," mean just that—N-O, no. You do not owe Little Johnny a reason. You do not have to continue a discussion with him. You can simply say, "No. We are not buying that today."

There's no emotion, difficulty or debate about it. Some situations in parenting can be extremely challenging. This one is not.

I have heard objections to this straightforward, no-nonsense approach.

"Well, what if Little Johnny has picked up the toy and has thrown his little body on the floor, kicking and screaming in the middle of the store?" First of all, if you know Little Johnny acts like that sometimes, you should put him in the shopping cart or stroller with the seatbelt fastened, before taking him into the store. Freely walking around the store with Mom or Dad is a privilege Little Johnny needs to *earn*.

But let's say this is a first-time incident, and that up until now, Little Johnny has been cooperative and compliant at the store. Assuming that he has already been fed and that he is not overtired (not a good idea to bring a tired, hungry little one into the store!), it is perfectly acceptable to extricate the toy out of Little Johnny's hands, put it back on the shelf, pick screaming Little Johnny up, and leave the store. This is not hard. It is an easy parental choice. Other parents who are watching will actually be amazed you have the guts to do this.

Why is it this type of abrupt exit rarely happens? Because *parenting by convenience* often wins out over *proactive parenting for long-term results*. Parents may be tempted to resort to arguing with their child because they perceive they don't have the time or the energy to leave the store without their errand accomplished. Unless a catastrophic meteor strikes, the store will be there tomorrow or the next day. Abandon your errands, leave the store with your screaming child tucked safely in your arms and come back another day (perhaps without Little Johnny).

Realize that being an emotional wimp by arguing with Little Johnny, whining back at him or allowing him to have the toy just because you want the confrontation to end is a choice that you own as a parent, and it will get you results that are similarly maddening in years to come.

I am not saying caving in once is going to ruin Little Johnny for life. The problem is, caving in once makes it much easier to slide into "cave mode" in the future. And Little Johnny now remembers he got his way once by throwing a fit; in his behavioral arsenal, he now views that as an effective tool to achieve his desired end...*the toy*. By introducing the protocol of giving in, you have started a training process—that is, one in which Little Johnny is training *you*. You may have extenuating circumstances, like an elderly parent in the hospital, or another sick child at home who requires immediate attention. It may just seem easier in the moment to give in and stop conflict. But ironically, stopping temporary conflict by caving in the moment creates ongoing conflict that will haunt you later. The pattern you set with your child when he is young determines the behavior he anticipates from you in the future. How you interact with your young child affects how you interact with him as a preteen. How you interact with him as a preteen affects how you interact with him as a teen. By demonstrating emotional strength from the start and flushing wishy-washiness down the toilet, you can establish healthy parental authority with your little one. Ultimately, that translates into the honoring of appropriate parental authority by your teen.

If you get tempted to be an emotional wimp with Little Johnny, because *you're* tired and hungry, or *you've* had a hard day, suck it up. Remember, you are the parent, and as the parent, you need to be mature, calm, and capable. If you are in a stressful situation with your child, no matter what his age, you need to be able to control *your* emotions, especially when your child hasn't fully learned to control his. Take a deep breath, remind yourself that you are the parent, and act like it. You will like the strong version of yourself better than a watered-down version of yourself.

As your child enters his teen years, you must be very accustomed to displaying parental fortitude in the face of conflict. In general, teens don't do well with nuanced communication. The best way to communicate with most teens is directly, especially when it comes to life lessons that the world will be less kind in teaching than you. A strong parent gives his teen the reality check he needs in a blunt, direct, firm, and yet loving way. After all, you are a "safe" audience. If you choose to handle your teen with kid gloves, continuously worried about offending him or saying something that will hurt his feelings or ego, you are actually doing him a disservice. His current and future bosses, professors and peers don't necessarily care about "being nice" or understanding his point of view. This is the stark reality of life. We must teach our children to have a "thick skin" and let comments that may be upsetting roll off their backs.

One of the harshest truths that the current social environment does not grasp is that while everyone may want to have a "say" in everything and be "heard", the truth of life for *all* of us is that *sometimes, what we think simply does not matter*. Every situation is *not* about us. We can have opinions; we can voice those opinions. But if your life boils down to a constant voicing of your opinion, then you lead a very self-centered life. And you likely don't make very much of an impact other than raising your own blood pressure and making people who are tired of repetitively hearing your thoughts "tune you out".

"What?!" you exclaim. "My opinions *do* matter. They matter very much!"

They matter to you. The reality is that sometimes all opinions – yours, mine, or your teen's – just don't matter on a macro scale. The truth is that sometimes, in certain situations, you will not *have* an opportunity to voice your opinion, or doing so may result in an undesired consequence like being fired from a job. When children can learn and accept this reality from a loving parent, it is much easier than learning it for the first time in a less forgiving environment.

7

Structure, Scheduling and Self-Regulation

Young Children Don't Get "Bored"

For many adults, structure equals boredom. However, young children love and thrive on structure and repetition. Little ones usually learn the concept of "boredom" when adults make the mistake of teaching them it. A routine schedule helps a child know what to expect and when to expect it. It helps her develop self-control and regulate her own behavior because it decreases her perceived uncertainty of this new game called "life." *Everything* in life is new to a small child! Imagine if everything you saw, felt, tasted or touched was completely new to you. A bit overwhelming to think about, right? That is the world of a child. As adults, we don't remember what continuous novelty was like. You might get tired of hearing the same joke 500 times, reading the same story 1000 times, or answering the same question 10,000 times, but little children do not tire of these activities. In fact, they *love* redundancy and need hyped-up repetition to learn.

Most importantly, recognize that your child does not engage in endless repetition to irritate you. It is simply her brain's way of learning and ensuring adequate repetition to lay down neural pathways of memory, experience and expectation.

Your child needs to learn what is expected of her and how to regulate her own behavior, but her attention threshold is very limited and her ability to self-regulate is underdeveloped. Learning self-regulation is not an overnight process. Indeed, it is a *lifelong discipline*. I am sure you are acquainted with full-grown adults who have not developed strong self-regulation skills!

Your job as a parent is to make it as simple as possible for your child to gradually learn self-regulation throughout her childhood and adolescence. When your child is a tiny infant, you create a regulated process of figuring out when she needs to eat, when she needs to sleep, and when she needs to play. This schedule should be as stable as possible, but not so rigid that it becomes inflexible. Don't become a slave to your child's schedule. Make it work for you, but keep in mind that maximizing consistency in your child's schedule will make daily life much easier for both you and your child. As she approaches adolescence, you nurture and encourage growth in self-regulation by coaching her through sound decision-making processes, allowing natural consequences for mistakes, and enforcing family rules.

Schedules Teach Children Values

It would be remiss of me to avoid mentioning that you should be prepared to tear your hair out on a fairly regular basis as you continually adapt to your child's growth patterns. No sooner will you have a good schedule figured out...than it will change. Your child will suddenly be hungry at different times, nap at different times, or be alert and playful at different times. This is completely normal, and it is a result of her developmental growth. Don't take it personally! Your child isn't "doing something" purposely to mess up your nicely organized schedule. Remember she is simply doing what every small human being is designed to do—grow and change constantly. And that is precisely why she needs the constancy and stability of *your calm presence* to help her navigate this otherwise new, confusing and chaotic world in which the slightest disruption can seem like a crisis.

With everything changing and swirling all around her, your child turns to you as her solid constant for unspoken and spoken guidance. She takes her cue on how to behave from watching and listening to *you*. If you act stressed and overwhelmed, *she* will act stressed and overwhelmed. If you act calm and cool, she still may act stressed and overwhelmed! She has not adequately learned to control or express her emotions yet. The world is full of things that she is trying to figure out, all at once. One of the best ways she does that is by watching what *you* do in various situations. Next, she imitates what she sees and what she is exposed to. Your child is a master of observation and imitation. She will learn what she lives. Guard the inputs of her life. What and who you expose her to will contribute to shaping her psyche—and her future.

A consistent schedule does not render a child-centric family structure. Ideally, the family structure should revolve around the family *unit*. Parents should establish their own adult roles and responsibilities to support family priorities and keep things running smoothly. Your child's activities are secondary in the family hierarchy of needs. Your child's needs should come after the family priorities, but before parental wants. With a little creativity, you can sometimes figure out a way to satisfy all three of those components—family priorities, your child's needs and parental desires.

When our children were small, my husband worked long hours, often not arriving home until after 8:00 p.m. Because our family priority was maximizing time together over having an early bedtime, our children went to bed later than most kids. Doing so allowed them to have time with Dad each evening. Our children treasured that family time, as we all did. Consistent evening family time was instrumental to the unity and cohesive development of our family. It was the glue that held us all together. The activities we pursued during family time varied depending on the seasons of the year and our children's changing interests. Some of our favorites included building with blocks, constructing jigsaw puzzles, playing guitar, listening to music together, going on bike rides and pond hikes, going fishing and romping outside. These evening activities were possible because we chose to modify our family's schedule to align with our family's priorities. Schedule modification was possible because I worked at home raising our children. It would have been a lot more challenging (but not necessarily impossible) if I had been leaving the house for work early each morning. As mentioned earlier, if you do *have* to leave your child in the care of others, make it an absolute priority to engage in interactive pursuits with her during the time you have together.

As our children grew, their interests and extracurricular pursuits shifted and our schedule changed once again. By this time, my husband had been working full time from home for a while, so our school days were punctuated by periodic visits from Dad. Because we were home together every day, interacting on a fairly regular basis, our family did not have an established dinner time. Our most meaningful times together were not centered around food and the dinner table, but rather, around outdoor sports and hobbies. Our children began participating in sports at ages nine and eleven. About this time, we purchased a house that required significant renovation, located 20 minutes from the home in which we lived. Thus began a lengthy era of bustling to and from sports practices, eating nutritious-packed dinners in the car and visiting Dad at the renovation site after activities. Often, our kids had dinner and took their showers in the functioning bathroom at the project house. Sometimes they helped Dad with renovation projects. Other times, we walked around looking at the neighborhood or Christmas lights. Frequently, Dad took a break from renovating and we lounged in lawn chairs in the family room to eat a portable meal. When we finally arrived back home, it was time for our children to brush their teeth and tumble into bed. The point is, we prioritized spending evenings together and morphed the children's schedules to allow this possibility.

In their early teen years (while still busy with sports and increasingly challenging academic schedules), our children had the opportunity to see the broader life benefits of prioritizing a fixed, but flexible schedule.

Their beloved Grampa was hospitalized for an extended period of time. During this challenging chapter in our family's life, we spent our evenings driving from sports to the hospital, meeting there as a family to support Grampa and Gramma. We visited, we laughed, we talked and we debated age-old questions of life and living. Our children experienced firsthand the fragility of life and saw through our actions spending time with Grampa and Gramma was more important than adhering to a specific bedtime or pursuing individual interests in the evenings. They observed how we quickly adapted our life schedule to our family's new circumstance, and this experience taught them a myriad of life lessons they carry with them to this day. It taught them the beauty of putting their grandparents' needs ahead of their own; to actively live with compassion, love, and adaptability; and that a meaningful life is largely determined by your generosity of spirit.

8

Feed Them Properly...Really!

Building Blocks

Food builds and powers your child's body and mind. A yummy and nutritious meal does much more than simply fill your child's tummy. The nutrients from a simple but wholesome, nutritious meal recharge his mind and body. The behavior, energy level, physical and mental health and even intellectual capability of your child are influenced (for better or worse) by what you feed him. The same holds true for adults. If you put junk into a body and mind, you can expect to get junk out of that body and mind. As I used to tell my children, "The foods you put into your mouth are the 'building blocks' that *make you*."

In a child, a suboptimal diet may manifest in hyper behavior, frequent illness, childhood obesity or learning and developmental issues. Obviously, these complex problems can have multiple causes. But diet—not medication—should be the starting point for trying to resolve these issues. Once established, a solid pattern of healthy eating can lead to a more accurate picture of what issues a child may actually have that are not related to poor nutrition.

The abundance of healthy eating alternatives, meal plans and even shopping lists at your fast-flying internet fingertips may seem overwhelming to navigate. In reality, healthy eating does not have to be expensive, nor is it difficult. It requires planning and some time. Above all, it requires a commitment on the part of the parent to prioritize healthy eating in the home. If a parent is not committed to eating nutritious food himself, then at minimum, he should be committed to feeding his child well.

This does not mean that "junk food" cannot ever be present in the home, nor does it mean your family's diet has to be perfect all the time. The goal is to have balanced nutrition from real foods, most of the time. Exceptions can be made, as long as they are just that—exceptions! And like any other behavior you wish to teach your child, positive role modeling is key. Your participation in healthy eating makes it much easier to interest your child in healthy food.

Begin When They are Very Young

If you start implementing healthy eating principles *from the very beginning*, you will encourage your child to make healthy food choices later on in life. Following a normal transition to solid foods, and barring any food allergies or health issues, your child can learn to enjoy a wide variety of whole foods at a very young age, with precautions taken to mash up or puree foods that he cannot yet chew or swallow safely (yes, I pureed lasagna). The more different tastes he is introduced to when very young, the better. And keep in mind if he doesn't like the taste or texture of a new food, all is not lost. Try introducing that same food in another month, three months or even six months and see if he likes it then.

If you set unhealthy precedents by catering to choosiness for a few years and *then* try to encourage food variety, it will be much more difficult, because palates become accustomed to certain tastes and textures. If you start late on food variety, your child will generally have a much longer list of "foods he doesn't like." This can easily be avoided, if you introduce *all kinds of different foods* as soon as your child has transitioned successfully from breastmilk or formula to solid foods. A child who is served "adult" foods (even if they are pureed) develops a palate that enjoys "adult" foods (especially if you don't replace the healthy meal with a hot dog when your child doesn't automatically gobble down the healthy meal). It is okay if your child doesn't stuff himself—or even eat—at a given meal. He will eat when he gets hungry. And if you consistently offer healthy food, he will indeed eat it when he is truly hungry.

Make Eating Fun!

Present foods to your child in exciting ways and you will be amazed at what he is willing to try! I often made "faces" on plates that caused my children to squeal in delight as they "ate the eyes" or "hair" of the featured food creature. A slice of whole grain bread with nut butter makes a great face. Black olives, cherry tomatoes, blueberries or cucumber slices make colorful eyes and noses. A mouth can be fashioned from raw green beans, celery sticks, strawberries or pepper slices. Apple slices can serve as ears, and a bow tie can be designed from raw baby carrots. For extra delight, make a crewcut with a light sprinkle of ice cream "jimmies".

Don't Force Them to Eat

I did not "force" my children to eat food, nor did I insist that they finish all the food on their plates. I served a wide variety of wholesome foods from the time they first started eating solids. After the initial phase of food introduction, they ate what we ate. I did not prepare separate "kid's meals" for them. (Illness was an exception. If one of my children was not feeling well, I made and served whatever nutritious food they wanted. Appetites are naturally affected when someone is sick. I understood that, acknowledged it and allowed for meal flexibility until they were feeling better.) When serving something new, I asked them to try one bite. Most of the time, they liked new foods. If there was a particular food that they didn't like after introducing it several times over an extended period of time (a year or so), I never insisted that they eat it. Most people have a few foods that they don't care for no matter what! For me, it is oysters. It's a texture thing. For one of my children, sauerkraut is a yucky food.

If your child is not interested in eating a particular meal, don't sweat it. Sometimes he may be ravenously hungry and you will be astonished at the vast quantity of food he can pack away; other times, he will go through stages when he seems barely hungry. The bottom line is—your child will eat the healthy food you serve if he is hungry enough. If one of my children was genuinely not hungry at a given meal, I would cover up the plate, refrigerate it and offer it at the next meal. Eventually, they became hungry enough to eat! Our pediatrician reassured me, "Sometimes kids will eat one string bean in a whole day! Don't worry—they won't starve themselves!"

Don't Be Overly Restrictive

Likewise, it is critical not to be overly restrictive and forbid your child to occasionally indulge in unhealthy foods. Having gooey, chocolate-laden pancakes once in a while at a restaurant is not going to create lasting nutritional problems! Indeed, quite the opposite—by nullifying the idea certain foods are "forbidden," you neuter food as a potential battle zone. Throughout your child's growing-up years, there will be plenty of behavioral hills to climb without making food a power struggle. If your child attends a birthday party or special event outside of the home, make sure he knows it is okay to enjoy pizza and cake if he wants to!

Planning birthday meals was always a much-anticipated event in our home. A few weeks prior to my children's birthdays, I periodically asked them what special foods they wanted for their birthday breakfast and dinner. They were allowed to choose their favorite foods in *any* configuration. That resulted in some crazy meal combinations served to Gramma and Grampa during their "birthday party dinners".

Our son's thirteenth birthday breakfast included whole dill pickles, blueberry French toast and palm hearts. Our daughter's eleventh birthday breakfast was berry medley yogurt and raw green beans. Not wild enough for you? Her eleventh birthday dinner menu included: crackers and seafood dip, kiwi fruit, couscous, rainbow goldfish crackers, brussels sprouts, chicken nuggets and cookie ice cream dessert. Pizza, radishes, an antipasto tray, crackers and the same cookie ice cream dessert highlighted our son's thirteenth birthday dinner!

What a Difference Food Can Make!

Our family experienced the life-changing effect of diet when our son was about five years old. He had been sick with back-to-back bronchitis and ear infections and had been administered two simultaneous courses of antibiotics as treatment for these bacterial infections. These were not prescribed frivolously by our pediatrician, but only after a period of time when it became apparent that he was not getting better and indeed, the bacterial infections were worsening. I fed our son a serving or two of good-quality yogurt each day during his illnesses, to help offset the negative impact of the antibiotics on his gut flora and immune system.

As a generally healthy youngster, he bounced back pretty quickly to his normal, bubbly self, interested in learning as much as he could about the magnificent world each day. Imagine my shock and concern a week or two later, when I found him sitting on the floor of his closet with the door closed and the light turned off. When I tried to engage him in conversation, he didn't smile or laugh as usual. He wasn't interested in doing much and seemed quite glum.

A couple of days later, I took him to the pediatrician, who also noticed his "depressive" state and ran some tests. After ruling out serious possibilities, the pediatrician recommended taking him to a neurologist for further evaluation. However, I had spent the past couple of days in extensive research regarding the possible impacts of antibiotics on the digestive systems of young children. I had learned that food intolerances or sensitivities could develop from medications because of the bacteria that were destroyed in the intestinal tract. Given that our son had taken two consecutive courses of antibiotics, I felt it was a distinct

possibility that his uncharacteristic behavior could actually be a symp-
tom of newly-manifested food sensitivities.

Our pediatrician was skeptical, but I felt pretty strongly about not
jumping to conclusions and immediately pursuing a medical/specialist
path. The fact our son's behavior had changed so drastically and in such
close proximity to repeated antibiotic usage seemed more than coinci-
dental to me.

The pediatrician and I had a good rapport, and he knew I was a dedicated and responsible mother. I told him I planned to first address our
son's condition with a drastically modified diet for the next two weeks.
If his behavior had not returned to normal at the end of that two-week
period, I would then pursue the neurologist recommendation.

For the next two weeks, my life became a non-stop blur cycling between running to the health food store, researching nutrition online
and experimenting with new foods and recipes. I pared back our homeschooling plans to accommodate the extra time required by me as "chef"
instead of "teacher". I also used this opportunity to teach our children
about the new foods we were eating. I did not burden them with all the
"whys" of what we were doing, so much as presenting this as a healthier
way of eating. I figured that since we had embarked on this unexpected
journey into the world of food sensitivities, I might as well use it as a
chance to turn the first page in their "nutrition knowledge" book.

What I discovered through educated trial-and-error was that our
son had become intolerant of all milk products and milk derivatives. He
also seemed intolerant of sugar in any significant quantity. After feeding him a diet containing very low sugar and absolutely no dairy products for two weeks, he returned to his normal, happy self. He was 100%
"back".

Prior to this experience, I would not have believed that food could
have such a tremendous effect on human behavior. Indeed, I knew our
pediatrician would have a hard time believing me over the phone, so I
actually made a follow-up appointment. Our amazed pediatrician saw
firsthand that our son was his normal and cheerful self once again. Despite his many years of practice, he shared with me that nutrition was

an area that most doctors did not have a great deal of training in. He also said that as a result of the experience with our son, he would certainly weigh food sensitivities more heavily as he diagnosed future patients.

For the next year-and-a-half or so, my son remained intolerant of all milk and most sugar products. Periodically, I would add small bits of dairy into his diet. These small amounts did not have any adverse effect. Those reintroductions gradually led to a full transition back to his normal diet. And our son was absolutely fine. His little body needed time to heal itself and did a fine job of that, without medical or neurological intervention.

I came out the other side of this unwelcome and stressful food foray with a little gray hair and a lot more knowledge on how to feed my family healthy, nutritious meals. After literally seeing the impact of diet on my child, there was no turning back. I knew that going forward, sound nutrition was as important to my children's well-being as homeschooling was to their education. Looking back, it was easy to see that our whole family was nutritionally better off because of our son's experience. And for that, I was and remain, incredibly grateful. We had been given "lemons" in the form of his health for a short period of time, but we turned it into "lemonade" (the kind without a lot of sugar, of course!)

Finding Foods to Fuel Your Children

Developing a flexible, nutritious meal plan requires a little creativity and a willingness to experiment. You may try some recipes that wind up being food flops with your family, and you will also score some unexpected home runs when you throw a quick meal together with leftovers (thinking, "here goes nothing!") and everyone clamors for more.

Spend time once a week planning meals, snacks and grocery lists. Focus on affordability, simplicity and adaptability as you map out the week's plan. Start with the basics: three nutritious meals a day that incorporate whole grains, good-for-you fats, protein, vegetables and fruit.

I also added in two snacks per day for our children—one late morning and one mid-afternoon. Because they were extremely active and played outdoors a lot, their bodies required these simple snacks between meals.

For our family, a typical day's meal plan looked like this:

Breakfast—approximately 7:30-8:00 a.m.
"Go-To" Favorite:

Oats mixed with plain yogurt and fruit, with a heavy sprinkle of cinnamon on top. As my children grew older, this transitioned to oats, nuts, cacao nibs, fruit, and milk. We called this favorite breakfast "snow," because sometimes I topped it with a large dollop of fresh whipped cream!

I recommend "old-fashioned" oats (instead of the quick-cooking kind), because of their superior texture. When my children were small and time was short, I didn't bother to cook the oats! I dumped a cup of uncooked oats into a cereal bowl, added some plain yogurt (whole milk, almond milk, goat milk, homemade, whatever kind of yogurt you like), and tossed in some fresh or frozen fruit (frozen blueberries were and continue to be a perennial favorite). I piled on the cinnamon and doused the whole bowl with fresh whipped cream! This breakfast ticks all of the nutrition boxes and takes less than five minutes to prepare. It also is very easy to teach your child to make this for himself when he is quite young. How wonderful is that—you will be simultaneously teaching him how to "cook" and getting a bit of a break from meal prep!

Morning snack—approximately 10:30-11:00 a.m.
"Go-To" Favorite:

Cheese sticks and fresh vegetables

My children's morning snacks usually consisted of a "good-for-you fat"/protein combo and a fresh vegetable or low-sugar fruit. For example, one or two mozzarella cheese sticks and carrot sticks or whole almonds and an apple.

Lunch—approximately 1-1:30 p.m.
"Go-To" Favorite:

Natural peanut/almond butter and all-fruit jam sandwiches on whole-grain bread, celery sticks, and fresh fruit.

Sometimes I substituted lean protein (tuna, chicken, fish or meat) for the nut butters and served the protein plain or prepared as a sandwich topping (tuna salad). Other times I served cooked vegetables like broccoli or cauliflower instead of raw veggies. A favorite strategy of mine that worked wonderfully for years was to put several pieces of raw spinach on the nut butter sandwiches. Even though my children weren't huge fans of raw spinach, they didn't mind it on their sandwiches. Nut butter yumminess overshadows a lot!

Afternoon snack—approximately 4:00-4:30 p.m.
"Go-To" Favorite:

Whole grain crackers and cheese with fresh fruit

Usually, my children's afternoon snacks consisted of whole grains, a "good-for-you fat"/protein combo and a fresh vegetable or low-sugar fruit. For example, whole-grain crackers and cheese, whole nuts (cashews, almonds, walnuts—whatever kind you'd like to try and is readily accessible), fruit or raw veggies.

Dinner—approximately 7:00-8:00 p.m.
"Go-To" Favorite:

Homemade whole grain pizza

Because we often went for evening bike rides, went fishing or played outside as a family until dark, I tried to keep dinners simple and portable. We often ate outside in order to maximize playtime. On these days, I stuck to healthy versions of quick meals, such as organic grass-fed or turkey hot dogs on whole-grain bread or buns, cooked broccoli and coleslaw. Homemade chicken fingers with peas and corn, chili, meatballs/meatloaf and homemade pizza were also favorite, "outdoor-friendly" meals.

Practical Tips

I bought a crockpot and used it regularly to create breakfasts (overnight steel cut oats and a baked apple dish we called "mud") and lunches/dinners (vegetable or beef stews, chili and barbecues). For several years, I made homemade yogurt in the crockpot, too.

By the time my children were between eight and ten years old, they had learned how to "construct" a variety of healthy dishes and snacks. As I planned meals each week, my main focus was preparing single ingredients that could be combined in many ways to create a variety of meals. I also learned to bake favorite muffins, breads and a deliciously easy egg pie, with a healthy twist.

A couple of times each week, I cooked large batches of plain quinoa, brown rice, beans (black, red, pinto, garbanzo— any kind you can imagine!) and fried or hard-boiled eggs. I washed a large quantity of fresh fruits and vegetables and stored them in separate containers without lids in the fridge or on the counter. When it was lunch time, my children made their own sandwiches or prepared a mixed bowl of beans, grains and cheese.

As my children grew into their teen years, I continued keeping *large* quantities of wholesome foods cooked and accessible. Because my children were athletes, they ate a lot! Keeping the fridge stocked with healthy food was a challenge, but it was well worth it.

I encouraged my children to think about food as fuel for their bodies, and I taught them to pay attention to their energy/productivity levels after eating different kinds of food. I encouraged them to make smart food-fuel choices, but I did not become "manic" about healthy eating to the point of forbidding occasional treats or criticizing choices they made when they were out of the house or with friends at activities. Because they grew up eating a wide variety of foods and had good nutrition modeled in our family, they understood that they were responsible for their food choices and their performance results. It was rewarding to see them learn to recognize the connection between food, physical and mental well-being and performance! Emphasizing healthy nutrition throughout my children's growing years contributed to their athletic and academic success and also imparted important, lifelong knowledge on how to eat simply and healthily.

9

Whoa Up on Diagnoses

Children Really Do Go Through "Stages"

Understandably, it is distressing when something seems wrong with your child, whether it be a learning issue, an injury or even a common cold. You want your child to be *okay*. You want her to be healthy and normal. You want to ease her pain when she is hurting. You are wired by parental instinct to protect, nurture and care for your offspring.

When something seems amiss with your child, it is tempting to seek an immediate "diagnosis," so that the "problem" can be quickly addressed. If you are working and time is scarce, the drive to fix your child's problem as fast as humanly possible is exacerbated. You see something is wrong; you don't have time or energy to deal with it; you want it fixed quickly and may be willing to literally pay to get that supposed quick fix.

If your washing machine or your car is malfunctioning, a quick fix might be great. But your child isn't a machine. She is a human being who goes through very real and acute developmental stages, both short-lived and long-lasting. If you are pressed for time, the alluring idea that a pill may instantly "cure" your child could seem like welcome relief from your worry.

Professional intervention may sometimes be needed; other times an extremely patient, calm and mature parent is the most beneficial prescription. The dedicated, nurturing parent understands that her parenting job is a long-term undertaking, not a short-term proposition. You can't rush your child's maturation. Each child has her own unique timetable for developing and growing. Even within the same family, siblings do not necessarily align with each other in terms of physical, mental, emotional, intellectual or spiritual growth. It takes many years of "two steps forward and three steps back" for your child to grow up. You may find that your child goes through multiple stages that she eventually outgrows, without external intervention.

As a mature parent, you can provide supportive guidance, affection, discipline and calmness to assist your child as she navigates the turbulence of natural developmental challenges. If you "whoa up" on the temptation to immediately assume the need for a "diagnosis" and first use your expert knowledge of your own child to coach her through growth stages, you may achieve the most healthy, desirable outcome for both your child and family.

As you consider your child's behavioral patterns, remember that the *industry* of "parenting help" has become a huge money maker. And just like with any industry, it is not wise to naively trust that parenting professionals always act with integrity. Many professionals *do* act with integrity, of course. But when you bring your child to a doctor, there is an understanding that you think "something is wrong" with her. The nature of doctors' training can create a bias in assuming physical or mental *medical* help is required to solve that problem. Certainly, medical help or diagnoses may be needed to help your child at times. But that is not *always* the case. As a discerning parent, remain patient and calm. Don't overreact and make things worse. And keep in mind that as a "worried parent," you may be vulnerable to jumping at a chance to quickly fix your child – but that may not be what is actually best for her.

10

Children are Not Mini-Adults!

Children are beautifully and largely transparent and present. They take each millisecond of life as it unfolds and devote their full attention to it. They impulsively burst forth with comments or exclamations without thinking about how their words will be received by others. Children revel in the joy of *being* and don't load the past in a backpack the way adults often do. Children are quick to laugh, quick to cry, quick to get over things that upset them and supremely easy to distract. They also love to repeat things—and hear the same things repeated—over and over and over again.

Stark Contrasts on the Playground

Go to a park and observe the distinguishing behaviors of adults and children on a playground. Adults usually occupy static positions on benches. They watch or sadly, keep occupied on their phones instead of interacting with their children. Some parents hover, especially if their young one is attempting a dangerous feat like climbing *up* the slide or hanging upside down on the monkey bars. Adults' conversation with their offspring features comments like "be careful" and somewhat rhetorical queries such as, "Isn't that too high for you to be climbing?" Sprinkled in between these concerns, you may hear a relieved but celebratory, "You did it!" or "Why don't you try it this way?"

Meanwhile, the children on our hypothetical playground participate in life at warp speed. They tear around chasing each other, fly off swings, clamber upside down over monkey bars and teeter precariously on balance beams. Actively engaged in their childhood business, they remain blissfully unaware of their hovering or sitting parents, definitely unaware of the tussle they had with their sibling that morning and oblivious to what might happen two hours from now. In other words, they are wholeheartedly being children.

Understand How They Think

It bears repeating because we so often forget it—children are *children*. Adults are *adults*. Children should not be expected to think, speak, or act like mini-adults. Adults should not think, speak or act like children. While this seems like a blinding glimpse of the obvious, it can be challenging to keep in the forefront of your mind during daily parenting. When you truly grasp the vast difference between the way your child and you think, act and see the world, you can shift your adult mindset to better understand the mind and behavior of your child.

It is easy—especially when you are sleep deprived—to slip into a pattern of attributing adult thoughts, motives and communication patterns to your child. Your child acts, speaks and interprets the world quite myopically. His mind revolves around himself, his needs and his wants. As an adult, you know that life and the world do not revolve around you. But your child hasn't learned that yet. That realization does not come until close to adulthood. Don't give up on trying to teach your child to be thoughtful of others; just don't expect him to fully internalize the concept of "otherness" or translate it naturally to his behavior before he is fairly mature in his thought and decision-making processes.

Get On the Floor and Into Their Worlds

Get down on the floor with your child at least once a day from the time he is an infant, so that you literally *see* what the world looks like from his vantage point. In an instant, you will be astounded at how amazing things look from ground level or even a foot or two off the floor. The underside of the kitchen table suddenly morphs into a beckoning fort. The sofa with the extended reclining footrest becomes a wormhole into the "hidden cave" under the sofa. Bookshelves adorned with colorful books most definitely look like ladders to a treasure trove. And adults simply look like giants.

Not only will this daily practice keep you physically nimble and delight your child, but it will also serve as a tangible reminder that your child thinks, speaks, acts and sees things *differently* from you. Think of your child as a puzzle to figure out or a gift to unwrap. He most definitely is *not* an adult. Don't expect him to be.

Respond, Don't React

Attributing an adult mindset to your child creates unrealistic expectations for him and can cause you to take things too seriously at times. When an otherwise discerning parent slips into the mistake of assuming that his child thinks like an adult, all sorts of bad things happen. If you do not keep the "child/adult" differential foremost in your mind when interacting with your child, you may find yourself *reacting* to your child's words and actions instead of *responding* to them.

Reactive parenting usually produces the opposite effect you desire. It assumes your child already knows how to act and speak like a mature adult. It assigns a seriousness to your child's words and actions, so that your feelings are hurt if your child says something nasty to you. The reactive parent may find himself drawn into an argument with his child, in which his parental behavior degenerates into childishness.

The business of life is hard enough for us to figure out and navigate as adults. Your child is certainly not equipped to do that at a young age. The wise parent who truly internalizes and "gets" this finds it much easier to stay in "responsive parenting realm," because he realizes that slipping into "reactive" mode is a childish tactic. His parental authority is diminished if he allows himself to be drawn into petty arguing with his child. If he allows himself to slip into reactive mode, the result is two immature individuals spouting off at one another—instead of one naturally immature child and a mature, patient, level-headed parent who brings adult perspective to the situation.

Be Cautious About "Reasoning" with Children

You cannot always "reason" with your child, because he is not *able* to reason like an adult. He will not learn good communication skills from you if you interact with him like his peers or siblings do. Furthermore, engaging in long "private" discussions to try to "convince" your child why his behavior or words are unacceptable may backfire—it can train your child to connect misbehavior with individualized, protracted attention from his parent. The fact that something negative prompted that special attention is lost on him. What your child will remember is that you stopped what you were doing, disengaged from other family members who were not misbehaving and swept him off to another room for a nice private visit. What a wonderful outcome of misbehavior! Instead of being temporarily removed from family society and placed in a separate room to illustrate that nastiness earns you alone time, your child learns that he is the "special one" when he is naughty. He quickly figures out that misbehavior earns him your undivided attention.

Additionally, emphasizing "private" correction versus simple and appropriate "public" correction removes the palpable benefit of correcting the errant one in front of your other wide-eyed children who are listening and learning by osmosis. One-on-one correction is sometimes warranted and desirable. But if the offense is one that can be handled more simply and swiftly by correcting your child as you prepare salad and stir pasta for supper, then use that opportunity to advertise to your other (behaving) youngsters what is acceptable and not acceptable.

This type of correction can be simple and unemotional: "Susie, you may not take toys away from Johnny. Please give the toy back to him now and tell him you are sorry. If you don't, I will put you in your room to play alone." If Susie does as you requested, she earns the privilege of continuing to play in family society. If she does not, stop what you are doing and administer the consequence as you stated. If need be, put a gate at the door to Susie's room to prevent her from leaving. Tell her you will check back with her in 15 minutes to see if she is ready to do the right thing. Then walk away (even if she is wailing and screaming), put a smile on your face and rejoin family society without emotional upset. And give your undivided attention to the ones who are behaving well.

Getting Sucked In

What does it look like when you inadvertently lose sight of the fact that your child is a *child* and get sucked into thinking he is a mini-adult? You begin to expect from your child that which he does not yet understand or have the capacity to give. You may expect your child to "give you a break" when you have had a hard day. You may expect your child to sit still for long periods of time (anything more than ten minutes can seem like an *eternity* to a healthy, well-fed, energetic child!)

Additionally, you may expect your child to remember he was told to not pull the cat's tail yesterday— or even an hour ago. You may take it personally if your child is grumpy or moody. Furthermore, you may expect your child to clean up after himself...because you told him to last week or even yesterday. When you begin to expect these types of adult consideration from a child who is not mature enough to deliver, you've backslid into the black hole of thinking you are parenting a mini-adult instead of a child. You have also forgotten that repetition is not only desirable but *necessary* for your child to learn.

You can ask another adult to please not leave the milk jug lid on loosely, and there is a good probability (but not a guarantee!) the adult will remember to tighten the lid going forward. Alas, this is not so with your child. Your child may need to be reminded of that task three or more times a day for months or longer. Additionally, realize that while your child may have left a path of toys strewn across the living room, he did not actually *intend* for you to trip over them and stub your toe. Take a deep breath and remind yourself of this fact prior to letting loose with an expletive and a loud, "haven't I told you 50 times to clean up your toys?!" The objective answer to that question is "why yes, you have." And accept that going forward, you will need to help and train your child to clean up his toys many, many, *many* more times before it becomes a learned behavior for him.

When you get frustrated with your child (and all of us do at times), try to remember that your child is not necessarily "uncaring"—another adult mindset. It very well may be that your child either does not remember what he is supposed to do or say, or he simply does not have it in the top of his thought queue. The "here-and-now" items are at the top of your child's list of Most Important Things, not the little inconveniences that can drive even the most patient and sane adult crazy at times.

Your child is focused on himself and what he wants to do. Your role is to gradually train him to understand that he is not the center of the known universe. This training process takes *years. Many years.* If you lose focus on the longevity of the parenting process, you may feel your young child's sole purpose in life is to send you packing to the funny farm. But I promise, it is not.

Recognize and embrace the little creature in your home for exactly what he is—a child trying to figure out how to *do* this thing called "life." *Respond, don't react* to your child's words or behavior. Even in circumstances when you don't have a lot of time to evaluate your response, you can still remind yourself that you are the adult and set the tone for calmness and maturity. Your child is closely watching you. How you respond to *him* will silently teach him how to respond to *you*, in both the short-term and the long-term. *Patient responsiveness* is key.

Stop and Breathe for a Moment

How does patient responsiveness translate into practice when your child starts throwing a major hissy fit for something seemingly insignificant? When your child erupts into a frenzy or shouts something unkind at you, don't react with an adult-sized volcanic eruption that dwarfs his own. Stop and take a deep breath. For ten seconds, consider the source. Consider his age. Consider his fatigue and hunger levels. Remember your long-term parenting goals. Recognize that your child may speak and act without thinking. If you need breathing room because *you* are tired or hungry, put your child in his room to play while you prepare a quick snack for both of you. After your snack, explain in simple, short sentences why his behavior or comment was inappropriate and walk your child through an appropriate, specific and modeled apology. Then forget about it, move on and go play outside together.

If your child is still having a hissy fit or screaming, leave him alone in his room until the storm has passed. He will eventually a) distract himself, b) exhaust himself and fall asleep, or c) forget about why he was upset in the first place. This process may take ten minutes or it may take two hours. At certain ages, it may be repeated multiple times each day. Either way, it will not damage him to have alone time to get over it. Put on some classical music or an audio story for your child to listen to near his room. Busy yourself doing some of the many tasks on your list or take a quick catnap. Check on him every few minutes. You will know when the sun has broken through the storm clouds and he is ready to re-enter family society.

Wear Them Out with Healthy Physical Activity

Your child needs to be romped like a puppy on a daily basis. Design your child's life to be as active as possible. Your child is not engineered for inactivity, nor is he designed to sit still all day. When healthy and well-fed, your child will be bursting with energy. He is wired to be running, jumping, crawling, climbing and exploring. Be cognizant and wise as you create your child's lifestyle to maximize activity and minimize sedentariness. In order to do this most effectively, *you* have to make time and be committed to engaging in active pursuits *with* your child whenever possible.

How can you nurture a high-activity atmosphere for you and your child without spending a lot of money or having a large outdoor play space? Big yards, parks and playgrounds are nice, but they are not required to create a rich environment that fosters active, imaginative play. You don't need a big house or room to plan "action zones" that stimulate your child's mind and body.

However, you do need to be willing to not have your home remain a perpetually perfect showplace. It shouldn't be a pigsty either, but let your child occasionally build forts under chairs or tables or in big boxes. Allow him to play with pots, pans and safe kitchen utensils. Take him outside as much as possible. Do not use normal weather fluctuations as an excuse to keep you and your child inside. If it is cold, bundle up. If it is hot, take water with you. If it is dark, bring a flashlight. If it is raining, put on raincoats and boots—or not. You and your child were designed to be waterproof. If encouraged by his playful, participating parent, your child will delight in rain and puddle play. Why is it that we are okay with taking a shower each day but for some crazy reason, we go to great lengths to avoid being rained on? Playing outside in the rain (sans thunderstorms) is one of the most wonderful things you can do to create lasting, happy childhood memories. And when you do venture out into the raindrops, be sure to bring your camera.

Have Fewer, More Important Rules

When it comes to establishing hard-and-fast rules for your child, remember that fewer is better, for both of you. The non-negotiable Big Important Rules that you decide on should be well-thought-through guidelines based on your moral values and long-term parenting goals. Rules should not be designed spontaneously to prevent nitpicky inconveniences that bother you.

If your child attends school outside the home, it is even more essential that you distill your family rules to the bare necessities so you help him learn obedience through *ease*. When your child has multiple sets of boundaries placed upon him throughout the day as he travels from home to school to aftercare to activities and then back home again, he can't keep track of all the dos and don'ts in a given day. Your role in training your child to follow family rules is to make it as clear and easy as possible, not to muddy the waters with a thousand inconsequential expectations.

Remember Growing Up is a Long-term Process

You may be tempted to expect abrupt, exponential increases in your child's maturity or independence, correlated to a certain age or grade. But your child may not mature that way. Cutting the cord strings of childhood is a gradual process spanning roughly two decades. The discerning parent lets out just enough slack as it is responsibly *earned*. Too much slack in the rope too early and your child will fall, because he didn't have the "climbing" skills he needed at that juncture. Too little slack and his next attempt to summit will be stymied because he has *earned* more responsibility by demonstrating his family's moral values, but he isn't being given leeway by an overprotective parent.

When a young adult perceives that he has earned leeway but is not being granted it, he may even rip out his pocket knife and cut the rope altogether, out of sheer frustration. When the rope is cut this way, a parent unfortunately loses his ability to coach and influence his young adult through the critically important early-adult years. Manage the parent-child cord strings wisely and you and your child will get to the top of Mount Maturity exuberantly and safely together.

Cultivate Obedience and Values Training

Cultivating age-appropriate obedience begins with first recognizing your child is not a mini-adult. The next step is to set your child up for success. Your parental interactions should reflect your understanding of the different roles of parent and child. Effective parental behavior does not degrade into pleading with or whining at children. Appropriate child behavior does not escalate into children dictating family rules or arguing about them with parents. As my mom and dad often told me when I was growing up, "When you have your own home and your own family, you can make whatever rules you want. This is our home and our rules, so you need to follow them." Short, sweet and oh, how to-the-point.

Direct communication is incredibly beneficial for children. They need to have a clear and healthy sense of parental authority. They need to understand appropriate roles for family members. If you do not teach your child to obey and respect your parental authority from the beginning, you set your whole family up for a lot of grief in the future.

"Obedience" today has a bad rap. Popular culture tends to resist the idea of training children to be obedient in favor of teaching them "individuality" and "self-expression" from infancy. Obedience, it is suggested, somehow smacks of imposing another's will and limiting "free expression." We are "supposed" to let our young children decide things for themselves and trust they somehow know how to make the "right" decisions even when they can't do addition and subtraction yet.

BAM! We spiral backward into the realm of treating children like mini-adults. The notion of allowing children to decide things for themselves presumes they have the background, knowledge and experience to know *how* to decide things for themselves.

Children do not emerge from the womb equipped with logical decision-making skills or life perspective. They arrive in this world as we all do, egotistically-focused and wanting to get their own way. Their worlds consist of themselves and what they want. What others want is beside the point. That takes all of childhood and often, a good deal of adulthood to learn. Even mature adults recognize their decision-making skills improve with the benefit of life experience and new challenges. And even mature adults struggle sometimes with making good choices or thinking about others.

Teaching obedience along with values helps your child construct a life road map with boundary markers and clear direction. Obedience training is one of the greatest gifts you can give your child. Teaching it requires a truckload of patience, calmness, resolve and consistency. As with most parenting responsibilities, it is a long-term, high-stakes proposition. Because it is exhaustingly repetitive, you will absolutely feel like you are futilely smashing your head into a brick wall at times. When you finally catch glimpses of unprompted obedience in your child, you may exhale tiny, hopeful puffs of relief, but those may be short-lived as she digresses into barbaric behavior a moment later. You won't fully see the most important results of teaching obedience (or neglecting it) until your child is much older. An obedient child learns to understand her role in the family. As she matures into a teen, this understanding translates into recognizing her role as a responsible adult in society.

Three Strikes and Mom or Dad is "Out"

Strangely, the baseball model of "three strikes and you're out" seems to be utilized by many parents as a "go-to" method of teaching "obedience". Theoretically, this strategy gives children three opportunities to choose to obey. Perhaps the hope is after parents repeat a request three times, it will be heeded? Put yourself in your child's shoes. Think like a child. If a seven-year-old "you" were happily engaged in an enjoyable activity (such as relentlessly teasing a younger sibling and delightedly watching the resulting electric response), and someone asked you to stop doing it, would you yield to them the third time they asked you to stop if no adverse consequence happened when you ignored them the first two times? Hmmm. Unlikely, I think.

In practicality, "three strikes and you're out" actually teaches your child she can disregard your request the first two times because *no corrective action is taken.* In other words, you *don't really mean what you say the first two times* because nothing happened when your child ignored you.

If you don't set the boundary and consequence up front for bad behavior and then calmly enforce it when needed the first time, you may expend purposeless vocal energy and simultaneously raise your blood pressure. Instead of keeping your cool, you may disintegrate into emotional upheaval, turn red in the face, raise your voice or act agitated. When your child misbehaves and you react emotionally, instead of rationally and calmly, you lose credibility and respect in the eyes of your child. Your child needs a firm, loving parent who says what she means, means what she says and confidently and fairly enforces family rules. There shouldn't be a lot of outward emotion about it. A matter-of-fact approach will more readily retain your child's respect and instill confidence that the family rules *are* to be followed.

Start Young – The Absorption Effect

Obedience and values training are best "caught, not taught." Small children can comprehend language at a much higher level than they can speak it. They are capable of understanding what we ask of them long before we often realize it! Young children also have an inherent desire to please their parents. This doesn't mean they want to do everything their parents ask them to do. It means they want a harmonious relationship with Dad and Mom.

Capitalize on that developmental stage by setting your child up to successfully obey from the beginning. Starting with your first child creates an absorption effect for subsequent younger children. Just as younger ones can learn their ABCs by hearing an older sibling sing the ABC song, so they can start to learn the dos and don'ts of behavior by watching the consequences that happen—or don't happen—when their older sibling obeys or disobeys. Younger ones often model their behavior after what they see "works" for the older one.

Values training builds progressively, with obedience as the fundamental foundation. It isn't impossible to turn the ship around if you start obedience training late. But it will make your job of teaching it—and your child's job of learning it—much more challenging. And truthfully, it may not have the same long-term results than if you had started from the beginning.

Choose Your Battles Wisely

In order to be a good parent, you must prioritize parenting. In order to teach obedience and values, you must prioritize your moral values and rules. If you want a peaceful home, you can't make everything a battle. You have to wisely consider which mountains you are willing to fight for. It's not hard to identify those peaks if you have already outlined your parenting goals (if you haven't, go back to the beginning of this book!)

Wise parenting goals center on the character you hope to nurture in your children, not on specific accomplishments you want them to achieve. As parents, we want to raise children who are good people. We want to proudly send them into the world, confident they will be net contributors, not net takers. We want them to use their gifts and talents, pursue their potential and propagate good as productive citizens. We want them to be independent adults, able to care for themselves financially, emotionally and otherwise. We want them to have positive relationships with other people, relationships in which they appreciate and respect and are appreciated and respected.

These parental hopes focus on human qualities and values we develop in our children. If you don't have extreme clarity regarding the human qualities you hope to nurture in your child, then it becomes very hard to distinguish—especially when your nerves are frayed and your child is in the midst of a meltdown—which obedience battles are worth fighting for and which ones simply are not important. The goal is to have few hills upon which you are willing to proverbially "die," those few areas of character that you have previously identified as critical ones to imbue in your child's character. These are your Big Important Rules (BIRs).

Determining fewer BIRs creates a higher degree of probability that you can consistently *enforce* your rules and that your child can successfully *learn* them. Likewise, whittling down the number of battles to fight sets both you and your child up for greater likelihood of success. The goal is not to "win," but to design a home environment that *effectively ushers your child toward alignment with family values*. The battle is not a petty competition between you and your child over the specific issue at hand; the battle is for their *future moral development*. Keeping that long-term perspective is vital for your success and sanity as you train your child to obey your BIRs.

In our family, we distilled BIRs down to the bare minimum. They reflected the foundations of character and moral development listed in the introduction of this book. Our absolutes were non-negotiable, age-appropriate and not up for debate. We as the parents (and in the best interest of our children) made decisions regarding which battles were worth fighting. In almost every other area, we strived to be remarkably flexible and fluid.

Realize your BIRs will change and grow along with your child. As she masters stages of moral and character development, your focus shifts to the next stage of the process. BIRs are not set in stone. Children learn obedience and develop values in a spiral fashion, not a purely sequential one. They will sometimes take two steps forward and five backwards. One child in your family may mature towards the next stage at age five, but another child in your family may not be ready for the next stage until age seven. The discerning parent who spends a lot of time interacting with her child will sense when each child is ready to move on. If it is the right timing, the progression will seem natural and attainable. If it seems like your child just can't handle the additional responsibilities, take a step back and try again in a few months. Don't fret if you tried too soon.

Big Important Rules – A Template

Here is an outline of our foundational family values at each stage of childhood, with specific examples of BIRs and selected illustrations of how that worked in actual parenting practice.

Little Ones (Ages One-Five)
Correlating Values: Obedience, Truthfulness
Big Important Rules:

- First-Time Obedience: When Dad or Mom ask you to do something, you do it the first time they ask (parental assistance usually accompanies the requested task to model the behavior or accomplish the task). When Dad or Mom ask you to not do something, you comply the first time they ask.
- Truthfulness: You tell the truth and do not lie.

Battles Worth Fighting:

- Your child takes a toy away from a sibling and refuses to give it back after you have instructed her to do so.
- Your child disregards your instruction to hold your hand in a store parking lot and pulls away from you.
- Your child breaks something in your home and then blames a sibling, hides the item or blatantly lies about it. If you are not 100% sure that your child is lying, do not ever correct her for it. If she did indeed lie, she may try it again and perhaps that time, you will have full certainty. If she did not lie, and you correct her for lying, the potential relational damage is greater than letting an isolated instance slide by if you are unsure.

Take a Chill Pill:

- When asked to clean up toys, your child puts one or two toys away and then gets distracted, not finishing the task. Come alongside her and make cleaning up a "together" game. Create a "clean-up song!" Most children need behavioral modeling for a *long* time before they can clean up by themselves without getting sidetracked. Getting distracted while cleaning up toys is their version of you surfing the net when you are supposed to be doing something else.
- You see a situation unfolding in which you know a lie will be tempting for your child. Diffuse it before that seed has a chance to grow. For example, "Susie, I saw you drop that cup. It looks like it might have a crack in it. Let's look at it together. If we can't fix it, we should throw it away so no one gets hurt." Don't purposely create conflict opportunity for your child by not addressing the situation in the moment, then ask her later about it to "see if" she will lie. That is setting her up. It's bad parenting. Instead, nip

temptation in the bud when you can to show your child truthfulness has good consequences and accidentally breaking a tangible item is not a big deal.

Middle Ages (Ages Six-Ten)
Correlating Values: Obedience, Truthfulness, Respect, Kindness, Self-Control
Big Important Rules:

- First-Time Obedience
- Truthfulness: You tell the truth and do not lie.
- By this age, first-time obedience and truthfulness should be fairly well-ingrained into your child's behavior. That doesn't mean she won't continue to test the rules! She most definitely will; this is normal behavior and should be expected throughout her middle years. Continue to calmly and consistently correct misbehavior as you did in the younger years.

In addition to obedience and truthfulness, many children in this age range are prepared to understand the following BIRs.

- Respect: You respect people, property and authority.
- Kindness: You show kindness to others.
- Self-Control: You exercise self-control in your words and actions.

Battles Worth Fighting:

- Your child purposely destroys or damages someone else's property.

One of the funniest disciplining stories in our family involved my children and our next-door-neighbor's playset. In our backyard, we had a wonderfully handcrafted playset, big trees to climb, a rope swing, a teepee and a zipline, so the two backyards *combined* offered an oasis of inspirational adventures for all of the neighborhood children. One warm summer morning, shortly after our neighbor's playset was installed, I brought a snack outside for our children. After visiting for a while, I left them to their merriment and went inside.

Later that afternoon, when my children were inside, I puttered out in the garden, trimming a few bushes. I noticed the dad and mom next door were busily sweeping and scrubbing the deck of their playset. From my viewpoint, it looked like a bunch of dirt was on the play deck. It seemed very strange, and yet, at the same time, I suddenly felt a bit of a hot flash. Had my children been involved in making the mess? I left my trimming and wandered inside. My son was vacuuming the house. After getting his attention, I asked him if he knew anything about the mess.

Oh, yes, he assured me. Both of my children had decided to play a "Tom Sawyer" prank on the neighbors. At the time, they were both enjoying fictional story books that vividly described childhood pranks. Apparently, they had cooked up this scheme thinking it would be a fun trick to play on the neighbors.

It was clear from talking with them that my children meant no ill intent, nor was the "prank" done maliciously. It truly was exactly what my son described—a childhood prank. At the same time, it was planned and purposeful. I wanted to nip this type of behavior in the bud with correction that would be impactful enough for my children to remember, yet appropriate in scale to the offense. Respect for property was the underlying principle I wanted to reinforce. The goal was to make this prank a one-time occurrence, so that they would know not to do this type of thing in the future.

I instructed my children to stop what they were doing, go next door and apologize to the parents, and then offer to help clean up the remaining mess. I quickly explained to them although they intended their actions as a prank, the result was that they had shown a lack of respect for our neighbor's property. Time was of the essence since I wanted them to get outside in time to help clean up, so my initial comments to them were brief.

Although it was embarrassing to admit they had made the mess, my children did as I asked. Our wonderful neighbors did not make a scene about it and let my children join in the remaining clean-up.

Later, I discussed the situation in further detail with my children and also circled back around with our neighbors. As adults, we privately laughed together at the incident, which left no lasting damage and resulted in a lot of quiet chuckles.

- Your child is purposely mean to siblings.

Our son had a penchant for placing not only *his* toys out of reach of his younger sister, but also *her* toys out of *her* reach! Despite my best efforts to teach him to share willingly with his sister, he struggled mightily to do so. As his sixth birthday approached with his hopeful expectation he would receive new toys, the problem seemed to intensify. One morning shortly before his birthday, I walked into the family room to find he had placed *every single toy* he could find on top of a bumper pool table, well out of reach of his toddler sister, who quietly sat on the floor under the table with wide eyes, sucking her fingers. That was the last straw. He was old enough to fully understand what he was doing and he had been corrected many times for not sharing. The consequence this time was ogre-like and unthinkable—we cancelled his birthday party with Gramma and Grampa. Thankfully, Gramma and Grampa completely understood and supported that decision. Instead of having them over for dinner and gift-giving, we had a quiet family dinner and cupcakes and stowed away the toys we had intended to give him until a future date when we thought he could handle sharing. While our son was not immediately perfect at sharing after that, the cancellation of his much-anticipated birthday party made a definitive impression on him, and that marked a significant positive turning point in his sharing behavior.

- When upset, your child does not control what they say or do.

Respect, kindness and self-control go hand in hand. You may be thinking, these "battle" items happen constantly and every day! To a certain extent, you are correct. This is when constant repetition and behavior modeling must seep into everyday life. This is when clarity about rules and consequences must be front and center in your thoughts. This is when you must keep your long-term goals in mind and not grow weary wondering if your child "will ever learn." Just as she learned to walk and talk, so she will learn positive values and corresponding behaviors *if you do your job with passionate dedication and do not give up on her.* If you are committed as a parent and determined to give your child the best effort you've got, things should turn out okay. Whatever you do, don't give up *now.* Your child is still incredibly reliant on you. You still exercise a great deal of influence and control over her daily life. Use that wisely.

Take a Chill Pill:

- You notice your child tends to be more disrespectful or less self-controlled when you travel, take time for vacation or host out-of-town company.

Children, as well as adults, feel more settled in their normal routines. As humans, we are naturally creatures of habit and find comfortable security in our daily routines. If your child's normal environment, eating or sleeping schedule suddenly changes, be prepared for her to test your rules more often. Ironically, misbehavior frequency often increases during these "special times" when we most want our children to behave well. Don't plan vacations with an idealistic notion your child will be an angel because it is the holiday season. Anticipate abrupt changes in her normal life may wreak havoc on her normally cherubic self. The same thing may happen to *you* when your schedule is topsy-turvy!

Go ahead and travel or have guests in your home! Do your best to keep things as stable as possible for your child when everything around her suddenly changes. She needs to know your BIRs are still the same *despite* changed locations or circumstances. She will test to see if you will enforce family rules when Uncle John, Aunt Sue and the cousins are around. Your child may even "amp up" testing you if she curiously notices that Uncle John and Aunt Sue don't seem to have similar family rules. Show her an extra measure of patience and understanding, but don't be a pushover.

Illness or injury can also cause a temporary blip in your child's behavior pattern for better or worse. When our children were sick, they often became unusually compliant and non-argumentative, which is the exact opposite of what I would have expected! Their level of cooperation served as a good barometer for their health; as they began to feel better, they also returned to being "handfuls." After I realized this was an unconscious pattern for both of them, I internally "welcomed" the return to their challenging selves, knowing this indicated they were well on the road to recovery.

Older Ages (Ages Eleven-Eighteen)
Correlating Values: Truthfulness, Respect, Cooperativeness, Thankfulness & Generosity, Kindness, Patience & Self-Control, Diligence
Big Important Rules:

- Truthfulness: You tell the truth and do not lie.
- Respect: You respect people, property and authority. You *earn* respect and trust from others by *being* respectable and trustworthy.
- Cooperativeness: You cooperate as a productive member of the family.
- Thankfulness & Generosity: You express gratitude toward others (including immediate family members) and are generous in sharing your talents.
- Kindness: You show kindness to people you know and people you don't know, when an appropriate opportunity arises.

- Patience & Self-Control: You exercise patience and self-control in your words and actions.
- Diligence: You work hard, even when you are doing something you don't particularly like doing. You understand that doing your best work reflects good character.

Battles Worth Fighting:

- Your teenager wants to learn to drive but has a pattern of mouthing off at you.

In our family, we highlighted the correlation between demonstrating respect in the home and respect outside of the home. If your young adult cannot control her temper well enough to speak respectfully to you, then she should not be operating a multiple-ton vehicle that can serve as an assault weapon in the absence of a controlled temper. Responsible driving is a privilege requiring significant maturity and responsibility. If your young adult does not see that correlation or argues against it, that also is a glaring indicator she is not mature enough to drive.

- Despite being capable of more, your teen does the bare minimum effort to get by in school but wants to go out with friends on the weekend.
- Your teen persists in building a pig sty in her bedroom, despite your requests to keep it cleaned up like the rest of the house.

During my children's teen years, I stopped by to visit a neighbor one day. The neighbor lamented to me her sixteen-year-old daughter refused to clean up her bedroom and attached bathroom and asked me to take a look and advise how I would handle the situation. When the door wedged open, I was shocked at the messy, unsanitary conditions before my eyes. It was like a pig sty! Before replying, I asked my neighbor if she wanted my honest opinion, to which she said an earnest, "Yes, please!"

I started with a question: "Who is paying the mortgage, you and your husband, or your daughter?" She reinforced my assumption that indeed, the adults in the family were paying the mortgage, not her child. To me, the answer was remarkably simple and straightforward. I told her something like this: "The rooms you allow your daughter to use in your home are actually *your* rooms. To the extent she earns the right to use them, they can be called and treated as 'her rooms'. But if she refuses to treat *your* property with respect, then she essentially becomes a tenant. When a landlord has a tenant who destroys property, the landlord takes action.

I would first establish a deadline by calmly telling my teen she had a week to clean up 'her' room(s). I would bring my teen into my bedroom and bathroom to show her an example of the neatness and cleanliness I expected in *my* home. I would then give her a 'punch list' of cleanup tasks to do in 'her' areas. By providing specific, itemized tasks, I would eliminate any confusion or opportunity for disagreement about what constituted 'cleaning up'.

Finally, I would explain if she cleaned up according to my expectations, all would be well and she would retain her belongings. If she did *not* clean up to my standards by the appointed date, then I would go into her room with trash bags and remove/clean up things myself. After that, the door to her room would be removed along with all unnecessary items. She would be left with a bed and a dresser. That way, there would be very few belongings with which to create a mess, so 'her' rooms would be easy for her to maintain to *my* standards! In time, she could earn back her furniture and belongings by consistently taking good care of the rooms and property in my house."

- When you arrive at the designated time to pick your teenager up from her activity, she keeps you waiting in the car without communicating to you she is running late.

It is understandable if your teen occasionally runs a few minutes late departing an activity. That happens to all of us and often is out of our control. But if she keeps you waiting an inordinate amount of time without communicating to you that she is running late, she has crossed the boundary into inconsideration and disrespect. Then it's time to chat and clarify expectations. If it happens repeatedly, your teen can cease participation in her activity for a timeframe of your choosing. After that, she can earn back the privilege of attending her activity by being considerate and responsible with *your* time.

Take a Chill Pill:

- Your hard-working and responsible young adult accidentally hits your house when she is learning to pull the car into the garage.

If you have driven long enough, chances are you have had one of those unfortunate and silly accidents when you knocked over a mailbox, hit a post you didn't see while backing up, or slid down the icy driveway into the garage door. It happens. Don't make a big deal of it. Get the car and/or house fixed and keep the story confidential to alleviate your teen's horror about the incident.

- Your teen tells you about a conflict she handled and is worried she did the wrong thing.
- Your teen confides in you she just found out her friend is drinking or doing drugs.

The fact your teen confided in you presents an excellent opportunity to not freak out and instead, to model adult problem-solving strategies. Her maturity in recognizing that adults may need to get involved for the sake of her friend's safety indicates that she may also be competent to brainstorm solutions to the problem. Stay calm. Ask her questions to help her think through the problem. Try to guide and influence her thought processes toward solutions that seem constructive for everyone involved and have the best interest of her friend's well-being in mind.

When disciplining and teaching values to children of all ages, the Big Important Rule for *parents* is to selectively and thoughtfully choose the battles worth fighting. Before engaging, make sure the issue is a hill you are willing to die on. Those hills should mirror the values you want to teach your children. They should be the "make-or-break" values that determine your child's future character.

If you correct *everything*, your child will lose respect for you because you fail to prioritize the important things. If you correct *nothing*, your child will lose respect for you, because you don't care enough about her to teach her right from wrong. Strike a common-sense balance that clearly illustrates what you see as the most important values to pass on to your child.

Be Doggedly Consistent & Repetitive

Once you decide on your family's Big Important Rules, commit to enforcing them consistently and repetitively.

Dad and Mom do not need to be carbon copies of each other and handle situations in identical ways. You may have a different parenting style from your significant other, but both of you should agree on the main rules, initial responses and tactical consequences for your child. You want to establish clarity and consistency regarding rules, positive consequences and negative consequences so that your child is not bogged down in a swamp of confusion. The goal is to maximize *clarity* in your family, so that everyone understands what is allowed, what is not allowed and what will happen if your child chooses to disobey. Clarity and consistency increase the probability your child will learn to obey as quickly as possible. Confusion and inconsistency decrease that probability.

If parents disagree on particular rules or consequences, they need to privately figure out a workable compromise so they can then communicate clearly with their child. It is not your child's job to wrack her brain trying to figure out the *real* rules and which parent really means business. That is unfair parenting and sets your child up for failure. How is your child supposed to figure out what is and isn't allowed if you as parents can't figure it out together? The only way she can do that is to constantly test each parent, to see what happens. If your child seems to be "playing" parents against each other, take a parental time out and analyze your rules and consequences. Usually, you will spot some inconsistencies between parents that your child has zeroed in on with laser-like precision.

Ideally, you should aim to create an environment that *maximizes clarity* for both you and your child regarding BIRs. There shouldn't be rule "surprises" that confuse your child. Clarity means you have established and regularly communicate your BIRs to your child in a simple, straightforward way: "This is the rule, this is the boundary and if you cross it, this will happen." She will learn your family values through repetition, repetition and more repetition. Rules must be repeated, moral values must be repeated and consequential results must be repeated over and *over* and **over** again. By now, you may have gathered repetition is a theme spanning all areas of parenting. Indeed. Without adequate repetition, your child will not learn *anything* properly. She is wired to learn through repetition.

Clarity, consistency and repetition in values training also *minimizes emotional reactivity during conflict.* Don't be overly emotional when correcting your child. If you have communicated consistently and repetitiously, your child will learn more quickly and relax into the rules. She will grow to understand that if she does "x," then "y" will occur. If she doesn't do "x," then "y" will not occur. If you have communicated your BIRs clearly and regularly, your child *knows* what the resulting consequence will be if she chooses to disobey. When the consequence happens, it should not be a "surprise" for her, nor should it be an emotional event for you. When codified as *simply* as possible and enforced as *consistently* as possible, BIRs maximize harmony within your family. And harmony within your family benefits both you and your child.

It's Much More than Obedience

The ultimate goal of teaching your child obedience to moral values is to mold her character, not just to have an obedient child. Be carefully cognizant of the battles you choose to fight and show her, by example, what priorities are important in life. The battle should never be a "battle of the wills" but a battle for *her future character*. In this regard, you need to resolve that your will to lovingly, patiently and firmly teach her will remain stronger than her will to disobey.

Because your child's thought processes are not those of a mature adult, she might sometimes think you are trying to "win." Fortunately, you know better. You know the stakes are high and her future hangs in the balance.

When your child is young, it is easy to establish "black-and-white" rules—the kind that have no "gray area" open for interpretation. As she moves toward her teen years, your focus should shift toward coaching and guiding her as she encounters moral dilemmas in her life. If you have parented well, transitioning to a guidance role while still maintaining "house rules" seems very natural and normal.

This is the time in your child's life when you need to spend lots of time *listening* and *talking* with her. This is the time when she can begin grasping that some rules are clear-cut, while others may have some "stretch room." As your teen starts to navigate the adult world, she will invariably notice many gray areas that she did not see before. A small child is not able to understand gray areas, which is why you need to do it for her. A responsible teen who demonstrates maturity and readiness for decision-making should be coached by her parent to think through the short, medium and long-term consequences of her choices.

Instead of becoming less important, the need for your parental guidance increases at the same time as your *actual decision-making* for your child decreases. As a parent-coach, you guide the *process* of demonstrating how to make wise, logical life decisions that focus on the long term.

You teach your teen to identify and weigh pros and cons of a situation. You stress long-term considerations, which remain difficult for many teens to focus on.

By deciding on your moral values and priorities, framing your family's BIRs to reflect those values and modifying your tactical approach to values training as your child matures, you can successfully help your child learn to make her *own* wise choices. *How* you teach her values influences *how she will decide on her own values* and put them into action in her adult life. Don't expect that your child will grow up to prioritize her values *exactly* as you do. If your adult child has sincerely thought through her moral values and priorities and lives her life in alignment with them, you have succeeded.

What About "Backtalk?"

One of the most frequent questions I hear from weary moms and dads overwhelmed with children's mouthiness is, "How do you stop them from talking back?"

In my experience, the best solution for minimizing backtalk is to address it as soon as your child realizes she can issue "no" as a controlling directive in her tiny universe. In my coaching and teaching, I have seen children as young as eighteen months to two years who are indisputable masters at definitively declaring a vehement, "no!" when they astutely perceive what is happening, or what is about to happen, does *not* fall into the realm of what they *want*.

You may be familiar with what happens next—if Mom or Dad does not "obey" the little one's directive, chaos breaks out. Sometimes, the parent tries to explain, argue or cajole her child into changing her mind. The little tyrant, on the other hand, has no intention of changing her mind and remains riveted on what is most important to her at that very critical moment in her existence. Outside observers might think the world as we know it is at stake as the screaming, whining, and tantrums ensue, perhaps from both child *and* parent.

As a supreme master of living in the moment, your young child may act as though she is utterly convinced with every conflict, the future of the universe hangs in the balance. Instead of trying to reason with her when she is much too young to be reasoned with, your role is to re-establish order in your child's micro-universe with confident authority. Cajoling, arguing with or threatening your child is not effective or helpful, and it usually exacerbates the situation.

Don't be tempted to whine back at your child. If you decide to provide her with a reason for not letting her do the particular thing she wants to do and she doesn't accept that reason, stop trying to explain yourself. Focus on confidently and calmly explaining the rule and correcting the backtalk. In our family, respect was a Big Important Rule. Backtalk is a manifestation of disrespect towards parents, so I began correcting it and correlating it to our moral value of respect when my children were very young.

If you start early enough, one of the best deterrents for future backtalk is training your child to be silent as a consequence for disrespectful words. My children grew up knowing if they spoke disrespectfully to Mom or Dad, they lost the privilege of speaking for a designated time period.

How in the world did I enforce this? By training them repetitively, *from the time they first verbally asserted their wills against mine.* At the beginning, the period of silent time was very short, commensurate with ability and age. I began with a fifteen-second interval. If during those few seconds, my children elicited a noise, I would correct them and reset the timer. When they had been silent successfully for fifteen seconds (which can seem like an *eternity* to a little one), I helped them say an appropriate and simple apology, "I'm sorry for talking back to you, Mommy." They got the idea quickly and soon were on their merry way to play.

As my children grew older, I adjusted the silent time upwards, to allow for a "cooling off" period. I knew the time was too short if, when they were allowed to speak after the first corrective time period, they immediately lapsed back into disrespectful talk or demeanor. It's pretty

easy to tell when children are still grudge-holding versus genuinely re-
pentant. I also used the time after these incidences to teach them calm,
respectful discussion skills. The goal wasn't to avoid conflict or discussing differences of opinion; the goal was to *avoid being disrespectful* in
the process. In order to learn how to disagree in a constructive manner, your child needs a loving, firm role model who knows how to work
through differences without loss of temper and yelling.

The value of this training expresses itself in its logical, beautiful simplicity—when you speak disrespectfully to Mom or Dad, you lose the
privilege of speaking for a period of time. Far from being oppressive,
this type of correction helps your child learn to control herself by not
speaking or acting on impulse, thereby avoiding unnecessary discipline
that she could have avoided. It helps her to succeed by teaching her to
stop and *think* about what she is going to say and *how* she is going to say
it *before* the words come out of her mouth.

As I corrected my children in this manner, I noticed it helped to
diffuse incidences that could have turned into serious misbehavior. The
period of silence halts the escalation of tension and if long enough, it
diffuses that tension, allowing for calm discussion. While helpful in the
younger years, this process is even more educational for your teen, as
she learns that practicing the moral value of respect extends to employers, mentors, teachers, coaches, peers and acquaintances.

One day, as I chauffeured my teens for the umpteenth time to and
from their sports practices, my fifteen-year-old daughter disagreed with
me about something and became upset. As she spoke, I could tell her
level of agitation was increasing. Simultaneously, she said something
disrespectful to me. I calmly stated, "Please be absolutely silent. Not one
sound. By speaking disrespectfully to me, you have lost the privilege of
speaking for ten minutes."

I probably was as surprised as she was to hear me say that! It had
been several years since I had employed the "silent correction." Because
I implemented it beginning when my children were toddlers, the need
to use it as a frequent correction came to a crescendo between the ages
of eight and thirteen years old, then dropped off dramatically as they

increasingly used their practiced diplomacy skills to disagree respect-fully.

What was even more notable was my teen's immediate reaction, which was to be quiet as requested (not a small feat for any agitated fifteen-year-old!) After repeating a second or third ten-minute interval (the first one was not long enough as evidenced by the fact she was still in disrespectful mode at the end of it), I told my daughter she was wel-come to join back in the conversation if she was ready to speak respect-fully. She was, and our day resumed its smooth course.

By using the silent period as a corrective tool, I helped my teen avoid further conflict escalation and practice self-discipline. My aim in the teen years was to make discipline as *effective* and *brief* as possible. Fig-uring out a correction that drives the moral value home and does so as effectively as possible ultimately means minimizing correction. Doing this takes creative thought and a great deal of understanding regarding how your child "works".

Later on, my teen and I talked about the incident. We sorted out whatever it was that she had been upset about in a productive and calm manner. We also discussed the silent correction and how effective it had been in helping her avoid getting in deeper tapioca. She mentioned when I told her to be silent (which I had not done in a very long time), it never occurred to her to continue talking. She knew how (and at this age, why) the process worked. In hindsight, she recognized by comply-ing, the benefits to her far outweighed the consequences she would have experienced by continuing to talk back.

You Will Make Mistakes

As you teach your child values, realize you will make mistakes. There will be days when you feel more short-tempered and days when you are more patient. There will be times when you keep your cool and days when you raise your voice and need to apologize to your child later. That is okay. You are human and your child is resilient. Thank goodness for that. Remember your parenting goals and the kind of human being you hope your child will become – and breathe.

Parenting is a refining process, not only for your child as you raise her well, but also for *you*. By parenting your child, you help her learn how to become a better person. By parenting your child, you *also* become a better person. When your child is grown and you emerge on the other side of your childrearing days, you may look back and be amazed at the growth that has occurred within *yourself*. I have changed and learned more than I possibly could have imagined from parenting my children. In many ways, it refined me from the inside out. Most significantly, I find that now, I *still* learn a lot as a parent. This time, it is from interacting with my adult children and watching them live their lives.

12

Let Them Compete, With Respect

Children Know the Score

One afternoon, when my children were seven and nine years old and playing outside with other neighborhood children (ages six through eleven), I witnessed a clear-cut incidence that illustrated how children understand and appreciate genuine, honest competition. A group of about ten children (mine included) had been outside in the heat for a couple of hours, so I decided to prepare some cool treats and surprise the hot, sweaty youngsters.

I gingerly opened the door, my arms juggling water bottles and orange juice popsicles. The late afternoon sun dappled through rows of sweeping oaks lining the neighborhood street. Located at the end of a quiet cul-de-sac, our driveway was the perfect start and finish line for every imaginable kind of childhood race, whether it was on foot, bike or unrecognizable home-constructed vehicle. Amidst laughter and shouts of, "I won!" came the inevitable wailing of race losers who weren't ready to concede defeat.

"But you cheated!"

"No, I didn't."

"Yes, you did. Your foot was over the starting line when she said, 'Go!'"

"No, my foot was right *here*, not *there*."

A couple of other children chimed in. "No, we saw it too! Your foot was way over the line at the start."

Putting my tray down on the trunk of the car, I overhead one of the older children suggest, "Why don't we run the race again? This time we'll make sure everyone is where they should be at the start."

Through a few more mumbles and grumbles, they reached consensus. There would be a "do-over." Staying near the entrance to the garage and away from the action, I settled in to watch the contest. I felt it was important for children at these ages to do their best to work through minor conflicts on their own. My goal was to stay out of it unless I saw things escalate to a point requiring adult intervention. The unfolding drama would be fascinating to watch.

"Okay now, line up your feet." One of the older children made sure all of the anxiously twitching feet were in their designated places as meticulously as if he were staging Olympic sprinters in starting blocks.

"Okay! Ready...set...go!"

The children morphed into gold medal hopefuls as they shot down the street. It was easy to see the race quickly boil down to two contenders as they touched down at the end of the street and streaked back to the finish line. Arms raised high as if triumphantly finishing a marathon, the winner tore across the finish line without slowing down and then began his "victory lap."

"I told you I won!" he called over his shoulder to the runner-up, who was the "toe violator" disputing the first race.

Still not ready to admit defeat, the runner-up burst out, "You cheated!" He quickly learned this was the wrong thing to say, as the remaining eight children all shot down his accusation.

"We ran it fair and square. He won and we lost. Don't be a poor sport!" I heard the sage advice waft up the driveway.

Sporting a sulky face like he was sucking on a lemon, the dissenter said, "Well, then I'm not going to play with you."

Without taunting and in a very matter-of-fact tone, one of the older kids said, "Well, it looks like everyone is going to play on the jungle gyms out back."

He looked at the group of children laughing and running around to the backyard. "I'm going to go with them. You're welcome to join us if you want to."

I walked around to the backyard in the opposite direction and was greeted by an excited, sweaty bunch clamoring to grab water and a popsicle. I moseyed around front and saw the sulker sitting under a tree. I guessed the lure of laughter and promise of tree climbing would soon propel him out of his funk and into the backyard.

Inside, I resumed my dishwashing and dinner preparations. A few minutes later, I glanced through the sliding glass doors and noticed the sulker had apparently meandered into the backyard on his own terms. Having realized his sulking hurt his *own* fun and certainly did not help him get his way, he had transformed into a happy, cheerful boy. The transfigured version of the sulker joyfully swung from a tree branch, echoing peals of laughter across the pond, along with his playmates.

Most children with whom I have interacted seem to have an innate sense of good-natured competitiveness and fairness. On many occasions, I have watched children in a group solve their own problems productively, without the need for adult intervention. This is not to say that children should be left *unsupervised* to solve their group dynamic conflicts. It simply means that if you stay as removed from the process as possible while still watching to make sure that nothing inappropriate occurs, you may be amazed at how your child and his friends strategize creative and fair solutions that mimic the real-world environment. And that includes allowing for healthy competition.

Everyone Is Not Always a Winner

During my children's growing-up years, a new trend developed in their respective sports that mirrored a more pervasive emerging cultural trend. Performance awards shifted to "participation awards". Both of my children competed in sports (tennis and gymnastics) that emphasized individual excellence and teamwork. My children experienced the winning *and* losing sides of matches and meets. They savored the sweet victory of triumph, standing high on the first-place block of the awards podium. Likewise, they learned the sinking disappointment of giving their best effort, losing and not being on the podium *at all*.

I encouraged my children to participate in a variety of competitive endeavors. Whether they emerged as a winner or a loser was not the point. The point was to *experience competition*—an inevitable part of life—and learn how to graciously win and lose. Even when they were disappointed by loss, I encouraged my children to reflect on the rewards of hard work and training that qualified them to compete. Many happy memories of practices with teammates and friends were another form of reward besides winning.

We discussed that sometimes your best effort isn't good enough to result in your victory. And yet, losing doesn't diminish those special memories, nor the effort expended to improve your personal performance. Working hard to achieve personal excellence creates tremendous intrinsic reward, even if you don't attain the highest level of achievement you had hoped for. I stressed the concept that in life, there usually will be someone who is better than you at something, and likewise, you usually will be better at something than someone else.

When the competitive nature of their sports began to shift towards "performance" awards, my children took note. What was this? The competitor who actually won the contest received a prize, but the loser received a trophy, too? Most of their sports friends noticed this paradigm shift too, and they were equally perplexed by it.

Unlike the adults who thought they were brilliant by inventing the idea of participation awards, the overall impression of the young athletes I encountered was by giving everyone an award, the *actual accomplishment* of the winner was watered down. The declaration of "multiple winners" diminished not only the true winner's achievement but also his effort. If *everyone* was going to get a trophy, what was the incentive to push oneself in physical training? Why bother training to win when winning wasn't recognized as being superior to losing? Although participating itself has many noteworthy qualities, it is not the *same* as winning. Equating winning, losing and participating demotivates striving for excellence.

It is important to allow your child the "trifecta" of experiences—participating, winning *and* losing. Learning to win and lose graciously is vital to the formation of strong moral character and is best taught through practical experience. Some children may *easily* win at a lot of activities. Others may *never* win but learn to have a great time striving. This is the inequivalence of life.

Remind your child (and yourself) we all can't be the best at everything. Sometimes we do our best and come out on top. Other times, we do our best and end up on the bottom rung of the ladder. Participating also creates intrinsic and extrinsic rewards—lifelong lessons that encourage us to stretch our character fabric, try new things and gain additional skills. But we don't need to eliminate traditional winning and losing in order to teach valuable life lessons from all three experiences.

Important Life Lessons

Nurturing a competitive spirit means fostering an environment that encourages healthy competition. Focus on teaching your child positive sportsmanship. Emphasize the work ethic of striving to do one's best, no matter what the outcome. When my children trained hard to excel in their sports, they expected to compete, challenge their personal best and maybe even win. They also developed a realistic perspective of their abilities, witnessing that in any competition, there were many "losers" and usually only a few "winners."

By contrast, neutering a competitive spirit aims to stamp out differences in individual performance. It creates a hyper-focus on participation *to the exclusion of* winning and losing. Excluding the idea of competing in an activity that is inherently competitive demotivates both effort and perseverance through challenges.

Not every activity your child participates in needs to be competitive in order to successfully nurture his competitive spirit. My children participated in many activities they enjoyed for the sheer sake of experience, learning or simply having fun. They approached these endeavors not expecting to compete, but expecting to participate and contribute.

You may wonder, what were my goals in encouraging my children to compete? I hoped that my children's competitive experiences, especially in athletics, would teach them how to...

- win and lose graciously and develop a resulting humble spirit (In my experience, most children need to be "taken down" a notch or two by losing in order to develop a genuine sense of humility);
- develop and demonstrate self-control in their words and actions, especially in the midst of frustration or discouragement;
- persevere and not quit, through adversity, pain and disappointment;
- train hard in practice, to the point of exhaustion, for the challenge of personal improvement (because practice represents more time than actual competition);
- respect coaches and those who knew more than they did about their sports;
- set goals, both individually and as a team member, and train incrementally, over a long period of time, to achieve those goals;
- rely on and rally around other people and teammates, encouraging them in their efforts and rejoicing in their accomplishments;
- translate their enjoyment into mentoring of younger athletes or philanthropic contribution to their sports.

Healthy and Unhealthy Competition

Within the family, a wise parent encourages healthy competition and discourages unhealthy competition. Unhealthy competition includes an emphasis on competing for parental attention or accolades, pitting children against each other academically, physically or otherwise, and directly or indirectly implying that the winner is more loved or appreciated.

This does not mean that children in a family can't compete against each other in neighborhood running races or family game time. Quite the opposite. Childhood races and family games offer informal environments for you to constructively model good sportsmanship. These healthy, bonding, competitive situations can morph into unhealthy ones if parents or siblings nastily taunt each other or imply that the "loser" is somehow "less than" in a game primarily designed for fun.

Healthy competition within families focuses on teamwork *and* individual effort. It teaches admiration for others' talents and skills. It celebrates the winner's triumph but doesn't diminish the worth of the loser. It teaches self-control, rejoicing in others' achievements and productively dealing with disappointment.

In our family, I emphasized healthy competition and focused on praising my children more for *demonstrating valued character attributes* instead of pure performance. Certainly, when one of them achieved a particular milestone, I recognized and celebrated that: "Wow! You won first place for balance beam! Awesome! You won the tennis tournament! You got a 98 on that math test—that's terrific! Good for you!" But more often, I looked for opportunities within their achievements and defeats to *praise their demonstration of excellent character*: "It was so exciting to see how you cheered your teammates on when it was their turn to do the floor exercise. I loved the way you showed good sportsmanship and encouraged your opponent at the end of the match, even though you didn't win. I bet your friend really appreciated the time you took to help him study for the math test. That really showed an others-orientation."

13

Set Up for Success, Not Conflict

Too many times to count, I have observed loving parents unintentionally set their children up for conflict, instead of success. If you believe that your child should be given choices in as many areas of life as possible, as young as possible, you place a burden of responsibility on your child before she is capable of bearing it. In other words, you set her up for conflict. By contrast, you can help your child transition over time to making her own age-appropriate decisions by teaching her the earned responsibility of choice in baby steps.

My rule of thumb question in determining when my children were ready to make any given decision for themselves was this: *"Is this choice in proportion to my child's logical decision-making skills, life experience and maturity?"*

If you expect your child to decide things when she doesn't have the logical decision-making skills, life experience and maturity to make a proper decision, you set her up for unnecessary frustration. Frustration and failure are important teachers. However, those dynamics will naturally permeate your child's life. There is no productive point in *creating purposeful failure* by allowing your child to make decisions she isn't ready to make.

Age-Appropriate Choices

Initially, age-appropriate decisions for your small child are occasional and inconsequential. As the parent, you should be making most of the decisions *for* your small child. Wake-up time, bed time, meals and snacks, clothing, and her basic schedule best remain in your purview of responsibility.

What kind of choices can your small child make? Think *very small*—pint-sized, like her. Your little one can choose her play toys from the selection you make available to her, her bed time stories and what stuffed animal she wants to take to bed, if any. Pretty much everything else is up to you.

Your small child is brand new to this world; you are not. You owe it to her to teach her how to make good decisions by modeling it for her for a long period of time. Through your thoughtful modeling, she can naturally learn how to regulate her activities and manage her own schedule, but that process is *years* in the making.

Some parents allow their small children to choose the next day's clothing; I did not. It was easier and more efficient to set out my children's clothing for the next day after they had gone to sleep. Because I planned our schedule, I knew the type of activities we would be engaged in throughout the following day, and I also checked the weather forecast. It seemed simple and logical to choose correlating outfits for them.

I didn't specifically forbid my children to choose their outfits; it never occurred to them, because they automatically dressed in whatever clothes awaited them when they woke up. Clothes were not a highlight of their day. They were too excited about getting up and creating another day full of adventure and discovery. I do not remember ever having a conflict with them about what to wear.

Once, when I shared my super simple "non-conflict" clothing process with another parent, I was actually asked, "Then how will they learn to choose their outfits?" After suppressing a chuckle, I assured the concerned, well-meaning mom I had a great deal of confidence the transition to choosing their own clothes each morning would happen quite naturally for my children.

Indeed, it did. And it happened the same way with both of them. One morning, when my children were about seven or eight years old, they wandered out into the kitchen with a different t-shirt and shorts in their hands. "Can I wear this instead?" "Of course," I replied. "You can choose your own clothes if you want. Just check outside to see what the weather is first." And that was the *entire* transition "process." No muss, no fuss, no conflict.

By contrast, I chatted with a mom who was bemoaning the temper tantrums her young daughter threw almost every morning about clothes. When I asked what clothing selection process she used, the mom explained she thought her daughter should be allowed to choose what she wanted to wear. Invariably, her daughter chose her favorite—a purple ballet tutu and cowboy boots. Now, if it was going to be a day at home, have at it. A purple tutu and cowboy boots are definitely an adventure in the making.

But unfortunately, this little girl also wanted to wear her favorite outfit to the grocery store. On a cold winter day. With no coat to cover up her pretty tutu. Or to the restaurant for Gramma's birthday party. Or to church. When mom said no, her little girl had a fit. Because she participated in a variety of activities, this dramatic scenario repeated multiple times each week. Mom admittedly—and understandably—felt frazzled and at her wit's end.

Do you see the conflict that Mom inadvertently *introduced* into her daughter's daily schedule? By giving her daughter the responsibility of making a choice she did not have the experience to make properly, Mom unthinkingly set her little one up for frustration and conflict. Mom gave her a choice...and then said no to her choice. How confused and frustrated her daughter must have been!

One way to know if you have mistakenly given your child too much decision-making responsibility is to watch her reaction to the increased responsibility. In this case, the little girl's temper tantrums were a blinking neon sign indicating that she wasn't ready for such responsibility. If Mom was determined to give her child a choice in clothing, she could have easily chosen two *appropriate* outfits and allowed her daughter to choose from the "mom-pre-selected" choices.

Coach Your Teens on Choices that Have Long-Term Life Impact

In the teen years, your child will make many decisions for herself as she earns that privilege. However, critical areas will remain where she needs guidance or coaching, especially as she thinks through decisions that impact her long-term future or require her to determine how best to live her values.

As a ninth grader, my son enjoyed tennis practice a lot. He enjoyed it a great deal *more* than doing his schoolwork. If it were up to him, most days he would have procrastinated doing his schoolwork until late at night, after tennis practice. Because we homeschooled, this would be akin to skipping classes in lieu of sports practice.

The family rule to prioritize academic work over extracurriculars quickly became "if you aren't done your schoolwork for the day, you don't go to sports practice." I didn't always implement this rule rigidly, because there was flexibility built into the spirit of the rule. My children had daily academic schedules outlining their classes and projects. The spirit of the family rule was that the large majority of schoolwork needed to be completed before sports practice, so that any remaining homework for the day could easily be accomplished after practice. By establishing this guideline, I encouraged my son to recognize his academic studies impacted his long-term future success much more significantly than tennis practice.

In tenth grade, my daughter 'decided' that she had had enough math. Her math requirements for graduation in our state had been completed; however, the rule I had established in our homeschool was that some kind of math class was required every semester, through the end of 12th grade. I made this rule when my children were still in grade school. Because I observed that math and science were becoming increasingly important subjects to master as technology catapulted throughout the world, I decided that it was important to expose my children to as much math as possible. I felt requiring more math could possibly increase future career options for them and would have virtually no downside. On the flip side, if they stopped math immediately after meeting state graduation requirements, I believed the repercussions could limit their career options, especially if they eventually decided to pursue a math-dependent field.

Additionally, I anticipated the possibility (or even probability!) my children might change their minds a few times before finalizing a college major. My priority was to keep as many future long-term options open for them as possible, so that when they did finally make their college major decision, they wouldn't be limited because of a short-term choice they made when they were in high school.

I offered my children a wide selection of math classes throughout high school; they could take classes up through advanced calculus and beyond, or they could take personal finance or business math courses. The bottom-line principle was, "Math is required during every semester through the end of twelfth grade." That rule was not negotiable.

My daughter ultimately chose to go a traditional math route and pursued a sequence of classes leading to calculus. During the last two years of high school, she became increasingly focused on a particular university which had stringent math requirements for admission. Even though she didn't like math at the end of tenth grade, she had the foresight to recognize that if she hoped to gain admission to her chosen university, she needed to change her mindset to enjoy math and do her best to excel in it. Through a lot of hard work and discipline, that is exactly what she did.

At university, my daughter subsequently chose a heavily math-dependent major that she became very passionate about. If I had "let her" stop math in tenth grade, two years before she entered university, she might have been too far behind in math to succeed in her eventual major.

14

Teach Them to Contribute

From the time your child is two to twelve years old, you possess a solid decade to teach him to contribute within your family and local community. With these skills, he stands poised to reach out beyond his immediate sphere of influence and contribute to the world.

What Can I Do for the World?

My goal was to recast my children's mindset from **"What can the world do for me?"** to **"What can I do for the world?"** This shift, from self-focus to others-orientation, occurred in small steps along a continuum that roughly corresponded to their young, middle and teen years. In our home, teaching contribution came with few words and a lot of osmosis. If you want your children to learn how to contribute, you have to first be a contributor yourself.

Your child's initial contributions will be small, but if you teach him to contribute within your family with tasks that match his capabilities, the significance of his contributions will parallel his burgeoning growth. Little ones are naturally fascinated with household objects such as brooms, dust mops, dust rags and pots and pans, especially when they see *you* using them. Capitalize on your child's curiosity about these household items and introduce him to cleaning as a toddler! As he follows you around, give him a small dust rag or let him "sweep" with the big broom.

I wanted my children to be proficient in virtually every household chore between the ages of ten and twelve. Not only did I think knowing how to efficiently take care of the interior and exterior of a home was a fundamental life competency, but also, it was a necessity due to the fact that I was juggling my role as mom with homeschooling. When my children were ages ten to sixteen, the majority of my time was dedicated to curricula planning, teaching, grading schoolwork, watching my children's sports practices and playing chauffeur as I drove them to and from extracurricular activities. As those years approached, I knew I would need their help in keeping our home neat, clean and somewhat organized. Therefore, the time for training them how to perform household tasks needed to occur *prior* to my busiest homeschool years.

Teaching my children how to dust, vacuum, help with landscape trimming, clean a bathroom or organize their bedrooms according to our family standards was time-consuming! I started working with them when they were about eight years old and taught them these chores one methodical step at a time. I wrote checklists, breaking down and sequencing the overall task into smaller mini-tasks; they referenced the lists as we worked side by side. On many occasions, I remember thinking, "I could do these things much faster by myself!" And indeed, sometimes I capitulated and silently crept into their rooms at night to clean out and organize their closets! (They were sound sleepers because they wore themselves out at sports practices.)

For the most part, however, I patiently worked alongside them as they mastered household skills at a snail's pace. By learning slowly and steadily, they internalized the process and also came to appreciate how their efforts helped our home and family life run more smoothly. I purposely paced the process, so as not to overwhelm them. My hope was they would not always dread their chores, but instead view them as opportunities to help. I aimed to nurture a cheerful spirit, a willingness to serve and empowerment to initiate helping in the home, not a negative attitude that considered chores drudgery to be avoided at all costs. By maintaining a positive personal attitude about household tasks, I strove to role model a service mentality for my children.

The Contribution Continuum

The timeline below illustrates age-appropriate contributions, using specific examples I employed to teach my children the habit of lifelong service. Their service contributions began in our home, then progressively expanded along with their abilities to include the community and beyond.

Ages Two-Five

- Supervised cleanup of one toy at a time
- Put dirty clothes in laundry bin
- Put trash in trash can
- Visit area nursing home with parent

Ages Six-Twelve

- Unsupervised toy cleanup
- Empty trash cans in house/take garbage bin to curb
- Empty dishwasher/help with food prep
- Begin learning household chores
- Visit area nursing home and participate by reading aloud, doing crafts and playing piano for residents

Ages Twelve and Up

- Independently dust/vacuum the home
- Independently sweep/mop floors
- Independently clean a bathroom
- Help with landscape maintenance
- Help with food prep

- Volunteer in the community
- Hold down a paying job while juggling high school academics and activities

Laminated "chore charts" were an *invaluable* tool during "contribution training" and served as reminder checklists for many years in our home. I simply hand wrote lists of routine jobs and tasks on notebook paper, laminated the lists and used dry erase markers to indicate what needed to be accomplished on a particular day. My children then used markers to check off the tasks they had completed. As their skills in food prep grew, I also laminated "menu lists" for breakfast, lunch, dinner and snacks, indicating the food options I had planned for each day. As you might imagine, my lists had lists! Organize your household chores and develop processes to streamline them with your child. It will result in a more peaceful home.

15

Teach Adaptability

"We're Going on a Daddy Hunt!"

I flipped on the hall light outside of my children's bedrooms and glanced at my watch. It was about 11:30 p.m., so I quickly calculated that I had fifteen minutes to get them up and ready to blast off on our late-night adventure.

I leaned over my warm, snuggly three-year-old son who was working hard at his sleep, nuzzled my face against his cheek and whispered, "It's time to go on a Daddy hunt." He roused awake. "Let's go to the bathroom and then I'll wake up your sister." Wide awake though still sleepy-eyed, he bounced out of bed, raring to go.

My one-year-old little girl lay sprawled in her crib, tiny arms flung out in a "T" shape, fast asleep. "Hey, sweetie," I said, gently picking her up. "We're going to find Daddy at the airport." She woke up a bit more slowly than her brother, but by the time I packed them both into the car a few minutes later, they were bright-eyed and excited, albeit a bit groggy.

Late-night "Daddy hunts" at the airport were a fixture in our life for a couple of years when my children were tiny. My husband's job required him to travel weekly, and he was usually gone Monday through Thursday. His flights arrived home late Thursday night, well after the children's bedtime. We drove as a family to the airport each week when he departed, and the three of us went to "find him" when he came home at the end of the week.

It might have been physically "easier" to have him drive to and from the airport by himself and let the children stay in bed asleep. However, the family priority of spending time together and actively showing appreciation for my husband's hard work and sacrifice in taking care of our family far outweighed any minor inconvenience. As a matter of fact, I didn't consider it an inconvenience at all. Just like we peppered him with hugs and goodbye kisses at the airport, so too we rejoiced in the excitement of his return home. It was an occasion to celebrate each week!

Not only did our "Daddy hunts" celebrate my husband's return home each week and show him how much we loved and appreciated him, but also, they were an opportunity to plant the seed of adaptability into my children's mindset. Adaptability breaks you and your child out of your normal way of doing things. It requires you to accept change and flexibly adjust to new, unexpected circumstances. I wanted to teach my children how to view change in a positive light. If you can teach your child (especially by your own example) to not only accept and welcome transitions, but also to *nimbly flex* and *thrive* during change, you equip her with strong mental agility for life.

Accept and Adapt

As I have said to my children many times, the most unhappy and frustrated individuals I have met are adults who have not learned to graciously accept and roll with everything life tosses their way. They muck through life, angry, frustrated or sad, because they can't control other people or get their own way. They sludge through their days stressed by uncontrollable circumstances, whether big or small. Even trivial things like a red traffic light can set them off. They fail to realize the inability to control circumstances and other people is a *universal* experience, and instead, they tend to think no one has it quite as bad as they do – either now, or in the past.

We *all* encounter people we wish we could change. We *all* experience uncontrollable circumstances—sometimes randomly, sometimes in a trickle or sometimes in a torrent. Life by its very nature is *uncertain*, and the adults I have met who have learned not only to adapt, but thrive despite that uncertainty, are the most productive and fulfilled people I know. They don't spend a lot of time railing about what is wrong with everyone else. They recognize the mindless futility of expending productive energy that way, so first and foremost, they quietly reflect on how they can improve their *own* attitudes and character and *take action* to do so.

That's why I wanted to nurture an adaptable spirit in my children. It is a discipline of the mind that reduces stress and maximizes potential. Plain and simple, adaptability is a *healthy* habit, both mentally and physically. As you reach out to the world with an others-orientation, you can simultaneously work to improve *yourself.* Because you hold the power to better yourself, your time and effort will be decidedly more fruitful than trying to improve other people over whom you have no control.

During my children's years of competitive sports and heavy extracurricular loads, they learned the inherent value of an adaptable spirit as our family faced the long-term hospitalization of Grampa. We rearranged out lives to prioritize daily hospital visits to see him, bringing love, support and laughter with us. Our schedule went topsy-turvy for a while, but Grampa and Gramma were our top priority. With creative juggling, we managed to weave school and teaching, work, sports and martial arts, miscellaneous extracurricular activities and normal household chores in between hospital visits.

The teen years are loaded with opportunities to teach and model adaptability. As their lives became more adult-like, my teens inevitably dealt with disappointment. I listened to and did not trivialize their concerns. At the same time, I sought to balance empathy with encouragement, reflective questions, and if appropriate, productive suggestions. I wanted my children to realize that the best way to deal with disappointment is to work *through* it, not *dwell on* it. Just like adaptability was vital in managing our busy schedules, so too mental agility was necessary to look beyond the transient disappointments of life and practice anticipating and adapting to change. By learning to practice the discipline of adaptability, my children became mentally strong individuals.

Whether your child does poorly on an exam, inadvertently gets in trouble with her boss at work or experiences the betrayal of a close friend, she needs your calm spirit, understanding ear and encouraging counsel. She needs you to be a wise and loving parent, who can help her navigate the specifics of her problem and gently instruct her in the process of growing through challenges by developing a resilient mindset.

16

Stop Taking Things Personally!

"Okay, take a deep breath and push up into down dog," I said turning my upside-down head sideways to check on my friend.

"Is this right?" she asked. "I can't straighten my knees all the way."

"That's fine. I keep mine a little bent, too," I reassured her. "Now inhale and..."

"He hates me."

"Huh?"

I wondered what realm our conversation had just popped into. Apparently, we had shape-shifted out of yoga and landed in another world.

"My son. He said he hates me, and it made me cry."

I sensed our yoga session may have come to a premature end.

"Why don't we work on some gentle stretching in a seated position?" I suggested, preparing mentally for the abrupt shift in topics. "Do you want to talk about it?"

My friend sat down heavily on her yoga mat and looked at me.

"I'm not sure what to do with him."

"Well, I'm not sure if I will be able to help, but I'll listen if you want to tell me what happened," I replied.

An hour or so later, I departed, looking forward to the walk home.

This particular friend was really struggling as a parent, and today was not the first time she had solicited my input regarding a difficult situation with her teen. I first listened, then reflected and asked her if she wanted my honest opinion, explaining I was asking because she might not like to hear what I had to say. After she assured me that she indeed *wanted* my candid opinion, I offered her my direct thoughts.

Have a Thick Skin

Remember your child—and even your teen—is not a full-grown adult. You need to have a thick skin and realize he doesn't always mean what he says—in the deep sense. If you feel hurt by his words or actions, don't fall apart in front of him. Put on your non-stick suit, let his words slide off and handle the situation objectively, with appropriate authority. He may actually be testing you to see how you react. Your teen needs you to model strong parental character. That means you must calmly and consistently set verbal and behavioral boundaries and doggedly enforce those rules. When your rules are violated, you must calmly communicate and administer consequences without being dragged into *his* emotional angst. As he interacts with the world and discovers that people and friends "out there" do not always care about him, he must be reassured by your actions that *you do* care about him enough to correct him when he is wrong.

If You Don't Want to Hear it When They're Older, Teach Them Not to Say It When They're Younger

When my children were young, I knew there were some words I wanted to teach them to use very sparingly. For example, in our family, we did not use obscenities and we only used the word "hate" once in a while, under specific circumstances.

I realize "hate" is often used as a synonym for "really dislike." But in my opinion "hate" carries a heaviness of negativity children can't fully grasp. Because of this, I taught my children to choose more accurate words instead of "hate" if they strongly disliked something.

For example, if one of them said, "I hate it when it rains," I simply reminded them that we should be very careful about using the word "hate." I explained that it was a very strong word, one that many people use rather flippantly, without thinking about or truly understanding what it means. Then I would suggest other ways of expressing the same sentiment, often in a more precise way. For example, "You could say, I don't like the rain very much, because we can't go outside to play. Or, boo! It's raining. I wish it were sunny right now. Or, I much prefer sunny weather to rainy weather." I also pointed out that we actually needed the rain to water the trees that we enjoyed climbing in our yard on sunny days.

Some of you may be thinking, "Oh, my goodness!" That is just word-smithing for no good reason."

I strongly disagree. The reason I chose to correct my youngsters when they used "hate" is because I did not want them to slip into an *easy habit* of using that word frequently or even daily. The reason I did not want them to get into that bad habit is because it seemed to me using the word "hate" often could nurture the development of a negative and disrespectful attitude. I did not want them to use that word against us as parents (or other people they loved) someday when they were teens and upset about a parental decision they didn't like. My principle was, "If You Don't Want to Hear it When They're Older, Teach Them Not to Say It When They're Younger."

I lumped obscenities into this category, too. When my children were an appropriate age (about the time they began daily team sport practices), I told them many of the obscenities they might hear *prior* to their actually hearing them. I did this, because I wanted them to know what these words were, what they meant and why we as a family chose not to use them. I explained with many thousands of words available to us in our native language, there were much better options to more accurately express ourselves than spouting out quick, over-used obscenities.

Teaching your young child to use certain words sparingly is *not* hard and can be done gently and conversationally. Trying to break him of the habit of using words that you have allowed him to use for years and *now* want him to stop using as a teen is much more difficult, but not impossible. Your teen might respond to gentle correction, but those chances are slim if he has been accustomed to venting, "I hate you," or other mean things to people without meaningful consequences. If he is not mature enough or calm enough to discuss why using these words is not appropriate, I suggest removing privileges and assigning additional chores for as long as it takes to change his language habits and his attitude. Lots of exercise helps, too.

Stress Relief the Healthy Way

On the family room floor near our kitchen, I designated a special place for a large whiteboard and a bunch of colored dry-erase markers. When my children were small, we used the whiteboard for all sorts of fun things. As they grew into their "testing" years, a Big Important List appeared one morning in the upper right corner of the board. Boldly outlined in black to remind my children not to erase it, the box contained one of my most valuable lists and remained on the board for several years. It read:

- 10 squats
- 10 jumping jacks
- 10 push-ups
- 10 stomach crunches
- 10 squat thrusts (burpees)
- 3 pull-ups
- 10 mountain climbers
- 30-second hollow body hold
- 60-seconds of running in place
- Run/walk 3 laps up and down the street

My Big Important List got a lot of exercise when my children were between six and twelve years old and daily testing the limits to see if they could speak to me disrespectfully. Yes, indeed. I used exercise as a correction.

A minor offense may have warranted my assignment of, "Do numbers one through three once." A more grievous offense might be rewarded with "Do two sets of numbers one through five and two number nines." And if one of my children (or sometimes both at the same time!) had superlatively chosen their words or actions poorly, they might have heard, "The entire list. Twice. Not another word until you are done. Go."

As my children matured (and got stronger), I used the exercise list less often. When I did need to use it, I increased the number of repetitions to suit their surging abilities. When they started practicing sports regularly, their stress energy was naturally released during practices. After sports practices, my children rarely had the energy to be contrary. Throughout the years, they saw through firsthand experience that one of the best ways of reducing stress was through physical romping and exercise of all kinds.

Because we were a physically active family, my children had absorbed positive associations with exercise from the time they were tiny. When they were infants, they enjoyed long walks in the stroller. As they grew, our outdoor activities expanded to include evening pond hikes, bug and butterfly hunts, bike rides and walks. We explored all manner of parks, forests and hiking trails together. Physical adventures bonded us as a family, so the foundation for enjoyment of movement was built from the time my children were very young.

While some moms I spoke to during those years thought I was horrible for "using exercise" to correct my children, I disagreed. I specifically used our exercise chart when my children did not treat me or another person respectfully. I wanted to teach my children how to use physical activity to burn off stress, instead of allowing them to develop the bad habit of lashing out at other people. Lashing out at others is an unhealthy and relationally destructive habit. If my children were upset or bothered enough to speak to me disrespectfully, then they *certainly* had enough energy to burn off in the form of exercise. Besides, I definitely felt better and calmer after exercise and I figured it would be the same for them.

In the end, it worked out just as I had hoped it would. My children did not develop a dislike of exercise. Quite the opposite. They learned the value of using productive physical movement at varying intensities for fitness, recreation, socialization and stress relief. They learned that exercise was way more productive than lashing out at other people when they felt stressed. And they learned that using exercise to relieve stress is a beneficial lifelong practice that reaps loads of health dividends.

17

"Parent" is Not Spelled "P-e-e-r"

Parent Now, Peer Later; Peer Now, Pay Later

The parents I have encountered who take their children's words and actions very personally are often the same ones who want so badly to be their teens' friends.

Allow me to offer you one critical maxim for parenting teens:

"Parent Now, Peer Later; Peer Now, Pay Later."

Memorize it. Plaster it on your refrigerator door. Reflect on it daily. Make sure your teen knows that your priority is to *parent* her now, *because* your goal is to be her friend when she reaches full adulthood. By reinforcing that idea, you can help her understand that you are on her side – that it is not "her against you."

If your teen is maturing well and respects your family values, you may share many moments with her that seem "friend-to-friend" instead of "parent-to-child." My teens and I pursued many common interests. We spent hours together doing martial arts, playing tennis, walking and riding bikes. We enjoyed deep philosophical discussions and theological debates. We spent hours in the car chatting as I chauffeured them to their extracurricular activities. And we shared loads of laughs and fun memories. The foundation which allowed these special times to begin surfacing as early as their teens was established long before they became teenagers.

Conflicts inevitably arose with my teens though, and at times, I had to make decisions that I knew were in their best interest, even though I *knew* they would disagree. I confidently made these calls. I didn't worry that my teens might get mad at me; I fully expected they *would* be mad at me sometimes. I didn't worry that they might not like me; I expected that, too.

Additionally, I expected them to remain respectful to me in their words and actions even if they felt mad at me or disliked my decisions. The "parent boundary" was still in place, even as we tottered toward the threshold of an adult peer-to-peer relationship. They knew that and I knew that.

The irony in the parent-to-peer teeter-totter is that to the extent you successfully maintain your role as parent throughout conflict, guiding your teen when it is necessary and judiciously exercising parental authority to make unpopular decisions when you have to, you simultaneously pave the way for a peaceful and rewarding transition to a peer relationship with your young adult. If you choose to be a peer too early, when what your teen really needs is a firm parent, you do her a disservice by abdicating your role prematurely.

Just like your younger child often took one step forward and three backward as she learned to handle additional responsibilities and make age-appropriate decisions for herself, so too your teen will wobble on the balance beam of teen-to-adult transition. Expect her to fall off sometimes. But let her try, especially if the decision she is wrestling with is not a "neck-breaker"—one that likely and adversely impacts her long-term options. Ask her perceptive questions and allow her the freedom to struggle through certain decisions. Encourage her to confidently take wise, non-impulsive next steps. If the result of her decision is not what she hoped for, she will learn from her mistake and gain new wisdom for next time. But if the decision point is a "neck-breaker" and she is *not* demonstrating rational, thoughtful maturity, that is the time that you step in as the confident parent who makes the call, whether or not your teen likes it.

For example, consider a scenario where your child may have a "D" grade in a middle school or high school class and is struggling to either understand the material or complete homework correctly and on time. What would you do if that child asked to hang out with friends on the weekend when she had a test in that class the following week?

There could be a range of appropriate parental responses, from saying "No, let's sit down together and figure out your homework," to "No, let's contact your teacher and ask how you can get extra help," to "No, let's call your friend Sarah, who seems to be a whiz-kid in this subject, and invite her over for pizza so the three of us can review together."

A responsible parent quickly realizes it is the *wrong* decision to prioritize *socializing* now over ensuring academic success for later. By contrast, the parent-peer who is more concerned about being her child's friend right now and who is not adequately focused on guiding and role modeling good choices for her child, would likely allow her child to prioritize socializing over academics.

The teen years can be a horribly frustrating time for your family if your teen thinks she is "beyond" parental authority and is running the show. But if you continue to persevere in parenting with love and firm discipline when she needs it most, the teen years can be a wonderful time of cementing the bonds you have with your young adult.

The contrasts between peers and parents are distinct, even if they may be somewhat subconscious to your teen.

- Peers come in and out of your child's life; parents are a reliable constant.
- Peers are over-emotional and often dramatic; parents are calm and steady.
- Peers sometimes react impetuously; parents are measured and thoughtful in their responses.
- Peers focus on popularity; parents know the decisions they make

and boundaries they set may result in their children disliking them for the time being.

- Peers think they are old enough to understand and handle adult relationships; parents realize *they* are still improving as adults.
- Peers may pressure each other to make bad decisions; parents encourage their children to do the right thing.
- Peers may follow "group think;" parents don't make their decisions based on what their teen's friend's parents are doing or are not doing.
- Peers may make decisions based on a "want" at that moment; parents keep long-term goals in mind.

When your teen reaches full adulthood, meaning she is supporting herself independently and is living on her own, you may be touched and surprised if she continues to seek your counsel in major decisions. This time, she understands that *she* will make the final call for herself, and she knows *you* know that. Because you faithfully parented her when she needed it the most, she now values your input and perspective.

And now, you can be friends.

18

Manage Exposure to Technology

Keep Their Computers in a Public Area

My children starting using computers when they were in third and fifth grades, as part of their core curriculum. The curriculum offered a structured computer/technology component that covered all the basics in a straightforward, thorough and fun manner. We had a small desk in the kitchen/family area of our home—the hub of activity. The computer my children used was the same one I used, and it was stationed at that desk. From grade school until the beginning of ninth grade, when they began virtual high school classes, that is the only computer that they used and the only location in which they used it. As they became more adept with keyboarding skills, they began to complete writing assignments on the computer. They also used spreadsheet software for certain assignments, as well as graphics software for drawing or creating slide shows. It was no secret to them that the computer was intentionally in a public venue in our home. They understood that whatever they were doing on the computer was not "private." The computer was a tool for schoolwork, as well as for limited recreation.

I loosely limited their free time on the computer, even for productive pursuits like creative writing. Because playing video games was not a "thing" in our home, I did not feel the need to be rigidly strict with time limitations. If my children had been interested in learning to *program* video games, I would have considered that a productive use of free computer time. Generally, I allowed them about an hour of free computer time if their school work was done and they had already played outside for a couple of hours. They didn't usually request time daily, especially as they became busy with after-school sports practices and arrived home well-exercised, worn out and ready for bed.

Don't Get Them a Cell Phone or Computer Until They Need One (Not Want One)

Your family circumstances will dictate when you feel it is appropriate to get your child a cell phone or computer, but the rule of thumb I suggest is, "Don't get them a phone or computer until they *need* it." Cell phones and computers should not be viewed as modern "rites of passage" that are conferred on children at a particular age. Instead, they can be used for either safety/critical communications with parents, or as utilitarian devices that are *earned* by showing responsibility and respect, with corresponding rules that need to be followed to *continue earning* the privilege of using them.

A fourth grader does not *need* to text with friends. A fifth grader does not *need* to post on social media or play video games. A sixth grader does not *need* to take selfies or send photos to friends. Those are all things your child may *learn to want*, because he sees "all his friends" and maybe even his parents doing it. As mentioned earlier, a responsible parent does not factor in what his child's friends or friend's parents are doing when considering the wisest decision for his own family. A responsible parent also wisely limits his *own* time on his cell phone, especially when his child is nearby. If your child is afraid of being "on the outs" or unpopular because he doesn't have a phone and can't text with his friends, then it is time for you to help him learn what friendship really is and what it isn't.

Likewise, your child does not *need* to watch movies or play with a tablet to keep occupied in the car. When you drive with your child, whether the distance is short or long, use the captive time productively to form family bonds and to teach him how to use his *brain* as an entertainment device. Play mental math games; play "I Spy;" play license plate games (looking for all the letters in the alphabet or all of the states); listen to music, a story, history, geography or science audios; or have special library books you save as "travel treats". These games, music and audios don't have to be continuously occurring during long driving trips. You can prepare ahead of time so there is quiet time in the car, too. Before long driving trips, I prepared special bags filled with inexpensive puzzles, toys, drawing pads and portable games from the local dollar store. I also put aside a few books we were given or purchased throughout the year to be used for future driving trips. Sometimes, we made a special trip to the library to get a huge bag full of books to bring on a trip. While there is nothing inherently wrong with having your child watch a movie in the car, I suggest you have it be a rare, special exception, instead of the norm. Don't squander an opportunity to teach your child how to entertain himself by *thinking*. You will create lasting memories and still laugh about them together in years to come.

My children got both their computers and cell phones in early ninth grade, because they were virtual high school students and *needed* to do coursework online and communicate regularly via phone with their teachers. They also brought their phones to sports practice, so that they could contact me if they needed to (these were the years when I dropped one of them off at practice, drove the other one to practice, drove back to pick up the first one after practice, and then drove to retrieve the second child! Whew!)

Even though they now had computers, my children were acutely aware their computers were to be used outside of their bedrooms – in the family room, class room, kitchen—pretty much anywhere except in their bedrooms. That was our house rule, and there was no argument about it. If the rule had been violated, I would have plopped their rear ends down at the kitchen table, stationed their computer at the table so the screen was visible to me, and revoked their "freedom of computer motion" privileges for as long as I felt it was necessary for them to grasp this was *not* a rule they should try breaking again. Probably at minimum I would have done this for two weeks, perhaps up to a month. If it happened a second time, it would likely have been for the rest of the semester.

Remember You Are Paying the Bills

When you provide your child with a computer or phone, remember *you* are still paying the bills. I strongly suggest you be the one to select, purchase and set up any desired controls on your child's technological devices. I also suggest you decline any phone or computer "gifts" from well-meaning or indulgent relatives. It is *not* in the best interest of your child to "own" his own phone or computer. It sets up a surefire scenario for family conflict if he misuses his device and you want to take it away for a period of time. If Grandma has gifted him a computer, you will probably hear, "You can't take *my* computer away from me." Now, of course you *can*, because he lives in your home and must follow your rules, regardless of who gave him a particular possession. But if you have purchased his technology, it helps to minimize this kind of conflict and the "righteous injustice" your child may vent if you do remove his devices from his possession because of broken rules.

One more note about family members or friends wanting to give your child electronic devices as gifts. Remember *you have the right and privilege to "just say no."* Inform your child this is a family rule. Furthermore, if you anticipate it might be necessary, be proactively upbeat—objectively and unemotionally inform generous people ahead of time that you don't allow technology items to be received by your child as gifts. Do not feel the need to explain your reasons, and do not get lassoed into a debate on the topic.

If this doesn't work, and persistent individuals blatantly buck your authority by giving devices as gifts, you have at least a couple of choices. First, you could return the gift, saying with a sweet smile, "I appreciate your thoughtfulness and consideration, but we don't allow electronic devices as gifts for our child." Second, you could say the same thing, with the addition of, "If you'd rather I keep the device, I will be happy to hang on to it until I feel he needs it. Or, if you'd like, I can return it to you."

I cannot underestimate the necessity of *not feeling obligated to justify your family rules to others*. Don't be emotional or reactive if relatives or friends challenge your rules. Just calmly state your rules, be confident in your decisions, and be prepared to set boundaries limiting visits or contact if these individuals simply do not respect your authority and decisions as parents.

Make Sure They Know It's Your Parental Responsibility to Check Up on Them if Warranted

Your technology-using child should be well aware that you have the parental responsibility to know what he is doing on his computer and phone, especially if he gives you cause for concern. He should not think he holds the ultimate control over "his" devices. As long as he is a minor living under your roof and being supported by you in any way, he remains obligated to abide by your rules.

At the same time, if your child is demonstrating good behavior, following family rules, performing well in school, keeping busy with extracurricular activities and displaying increasing maturity in character development, don't check up on him for no apparent reason other than curiosity. My children knew our family rules very well because I frequently communicated those rules in a positive way. They also knew that I respected their privacy and trusted they were following the rules. They knew that if I had sensed something to be concerned about, I would have checked up on their phone or computer usage or even gone through their school bags or closets. As my children showed increasing responsibility, I extended this trust to them. If they had breached that trust in a significant way, the consequences would have been equally significant and also, long-lasting.

Manage It or They Will Manage You

Your child benefits if you establish easy-to-understand, broad brush stroke principles for managing technology in your home. Consider the following strategies as you determine parameters for your child's screen and device usage.

Establish your rules and communicate them clearly and positively *prior* to providing your child with any devices. He should not be expected to read your mind to try to figure out the rules. Don't first give the privilege of device usage and then wait until there is a problem before setting ground rules. If you communicate beforehand and your child chooses to break a rule, it indeed represents his *choice*. Articulate your rules on a regular basis and post them visibly in your home as a constant reminder. Remember that your child (who is not a mini-adult) needs to be frequently reminded of many things!

With devices, the "less is more" adage was my preference. Technology is not going away and your child is bombarded with screens and devices on a daily basis. Help him learn early in life to strike a reasonable balance between screen time of all kinds, and the action of real life, which moves at a different pace and intensity. For example, in real life, we hear sounds of nature or environmental surroundings, not fast-paced action music or suspenseful, dramatic music as we move through our days or talk with family members!

Consider not allowing video games in your home. Believe it or not, your child really can grow up and be better off without ever having played video games in your home. If you decide you want to allow video games in your home, carefully monitor their usage. If you decide not to have video games in your home, you could occasionally take your child to an arcade for a fun outing.

Don't fall prey to thinking that your child will somehow be "behind" in knowing how to use computers if he isn't constantly using them while growing up. Computers will be part of his academic and personal life, likely for the rest of his life. He can learn really fast. He won't be behind the eight ball if you don't get him the latest and greatest devices.

Along with communicating your technology rules, communicate specifically what the consequences will be if your child breaks the rules. I have found the most effective consequences (for any kind of misbehavior, not just offenses related to technology) are ones that are *directly related to the offense* and involve *a time period that is significant enough to alter future behavior*. For example, losing the privilege of using one's phone for a day may not be a significant enough time period to encourage altered future behavior for many teens. It is barely a light tap to the wrist. Losing one's phone for a minimum of a week, however...now *that* would be quite traumatic for many teens. Point being, if your teen lost his phone for a week *once*, he would probably think *twice* before breaking the rules again. Remember, your goal is not to mete out ongoing consequences. Quite the contrary. You want your child to *succeed* in demonstrating respect for the rules you have established, whether he likes them or not. Tell him that before he breaks any technology rules.

If your child breaks your rules, follow through with the consequences you have communicated. Do not be wishy-washy and give second and third chances. If you do, you are teaching him that you do not mean what you say. Your firm hand in implementing stated consequences is as important as making the consequence an appropriately significant one. Don't set your family up for dragged out conflict scenarios by giving in or watering down consequences until they are meaningless. That is *not* the goal of correction. If your child seems to be breaking the same rule consistently, strengthen and shore up your consequences to minimize future infractions.

19

Teach Strength in Adversity

Out of the Mouth of My Mom

My parents had a simple, practical and no-nonsense approach to life, parenting and overcoming adversity. Especially when I was a teen, they didn't belabor correction and open the door for argumentative conflict with long-winded explanations or justifications for their rules. In particular, my mom had a series of objective, go-to adages that regularly peppered her communication with me. As a young adult, I had not realized that these sayings were actually stuffed with straightforward wisdom. And yet, years later as a mom, I suddenly understood the inherent value of keeping things short and sweet. In fact, I was amazed at how often my mom's go-to cliches popped into my mind – and mouth – at opportune moments with my own children.

Some of my mom's favorites included:

"If you don't have anything nice to say, don't say anything at all."

"You'll never know if you can do it until you try."

"If at first you don't succeed, try, try again."

And the one I cringed most at hearing when I was a teen...

"This is our home and our rules. So long as you live here, you will follow our rules respectfully. When you have your own home, you can make your own rules."

Overcome, Don't Give Up

My parents encouraged me to push my limits on a regular basis—in sports, in academics, in work and in life. They didn't fret when I was practicing the next progressive acrobatic skill on the balance beam. They didn't try to protect me from taking a heavier course load that would mean more homework, less free time and not guarantee all "A" grades for the semester. They didn't discourage me from working during the school year because I might not have enough time to study or sleep.

Born at the beginning of the Great Depression in 1930, Mom and Dad clearly remembered what real hardship was. They grew up watching their parents struggle to feed their families. When they were nine years old, World War II broke out. Far from being footloose and fancy free, Mom and Dad's preteen and teen years involved personal sacrifice, as they helped to financially support their families. In hindsight, I think *their* experiences overcoming adversity established a healthy threshold for their faith in *my* ability to figure out how to work through difficulties. They viewed adversity as a normal and healthy part of growing up, not something to protect their children from at all costs. By example, Dad and Mom taught me to set my own expectation bar high, work hard to reach it and then, raise it a little higher. They taught me this kind of incremental but constant growth would enable me to accomplish things I never dreamed of. They emboldened me to thoughtfully calculate future risk but not be afraid to step out into the unknown.

By challenging myself, I learned true confidence doesn't come from the external environment or from other people around you. Confidence in yourself develops from *within*, as you push yourself and realize you are far more capable than you had thought. It gives rise to the self-belief that even if you encounter a problem with which you have no experience or cannot readily see obvious solutions, you *can* figure it out with creative determination.

Get a Real Job

Just as I think competitive sports imparts lessons children cannot learn quite the same way through other means, so too I think holding down a "real" job imparts critical lessons for a lifetime.

When I was a teen, working part-time while juggling schoolwork, sports, volunteering and other extracurriculars was the norm. Most of my peers had part-time jobs during the academic year, squeezed in after evening sports practices or on the weekends. By February of each year, my friends and I were also hot on the search for full-time summer jobs. I don't remember a lot of discussion about the *types* of summer jobs we were seeking. The goal was to get a job—*any* job—to earn money to help pay for college, enjoy a bit of spending money and save for our futures. We recognized that virtually any kind of work experience would increase our marketable skills (and that we possessed few, if any, marketable skills as high school students!). We weren't choosy. We looked forward to the chance to earn money by working hard.

A paying job teaches lessons that volunteer work simply cannot. If you oversleep for a volunteer engagement, there is no risk that a permanent "terminated" might be emblazoned across your employment history. If you don't particularly like a volunteer position or individual you encounter, you can get up and leave with little to no accountability or adverse consequences. Volunteering is a tremendously worthwhile pursuit and has its own laudable merits. My children and I participated in numerous volunteer activities throughout their growing-up years.

But a job is different. A job teaches your child:

- The importance of being a net contributor – more than a societal consumer;
- The "value of a dollar";

It is hard for your child to fully grasp the worth of money until she is working hard to earn it, and then she sees firsthand how much smaller her paycheck is than she expected it to be due to taxes. It is one thing to know this intellectually; it is a *very different* thing to see it actually *happen.*

- Accountability for satisfactory performance despite how she might *feel* on a particular day or how she might feel about the tasks she is required to carry out;

Learning to "suck it up" and show a cheerful face on the outside even if she feels like complaining on the inside is a productive lesson for your child in perseverance and disciplining herself to be positive.

- Poor job performance can lead to long-lasting consequences;

If your child gets fired from a job due to negligence, lack of punctuality or insubordination, she may have a hard time explaining that termination in the future as she applies for other jobs.

- How demonstrating a strong, consistent work ethic develops her character and confidence;
- Personal pride and discipline in doing her best no matter how "menial" or messy the task happens to be;
- How to step up to the plate when challenged with new responsibility;
- Humility in starting at the *bottom* with a low-level entry position and understanding through experience that no job is "beneath" her;

Some of the messiest "grunt work" is noble, meaningful and vitally necessary.

- Productivity versus idleness;

Social media, video games and hanging out, while not problematic in small doses, often feed the insidious habit of idleness.

- Multitasking and prioritization;

I have observed that teens who stay really busy with school, work, and other productive pursuits have little time and even less motivation to get into trouble.

- Sometimes, your teen just needs to keep her mouth shut and *not* express her opinion.

When she is hired to do a job as a teen, her focus should be on performing her best, instead of finding flaws in her peers' performance. Your teen will see through experience that it is not always appropriate to voice her thoughts or opinions regarding what she does or doesn't like about the job, the organization or her co-workers. Employers don't hire teens to critique their business practices. They hire them to do a job. This can be a hard pill for your teen to swallow, but it is very helpful in teaching her not to demonstrate a superior attitude, which is better to learn earlier in life rather than later.

As teens, both of my children worked for the local grocery store, a large regional chain with a solid training program for new hires. After completing the training and beginning shift work in the store, my teens mentioned one of their rotating duties included cleaning the public restrooms (because they had learned to clean our home bathrooms when fairly young, it didn't faze them too much). When I heard this news, I couldn't have been more delighted. I remember matter-of-factly commenting, "Well, that's a menial task, but it's pretty important." On the inside, however, I was jumping up and down and cheering!

One of my young adult jobs had been equally messy, mentally challenging and physically exhausting. That job taught me more about life and myself than any other position I ever held. Likewise, it motivated me to set ambitious future goals and attack them with gusto. Thus, my automatic reaction upon hearing about the store's bathroom cleaning requirement was, strangely enough, excitement and positivity. I knew my teens would learn humility on the job in a way that I couldn't possibly teach them. They would take pride in transforming a dirty bathroom into a shining one (as they did at home) and demonstrate a strong work ethic in the midst of an undesirable task. Most importantly, they would learn through experience that every legitimate job is a noble job if you approach it with a positive attitude and determination to succeed.

Teach Logical Thinking and Decision-Making Skills

Teach your child logical thinking skills and help her learn the process of making grounded, objective, balanced decisions. While emotion may be a relevant factor in decision making, my experience with teens has been that their emotions sometimes overrun their logic, especially when they are upset. Your teen needs your calm, rational coaching on *how* to make sound, principled decisions, so that with time and practice, she hones a transferable decision-making skill set.

I taught my children logic beginning when they were young, by using fun workbooks. This led to a more formal year of logic study in eighth grade. From that point on, our logic training transitioned from academic to real-life application. As situations arose throughout their high school years, we jointly considered solutions using the basic foundations of logic they had learned since they were young.

Instead of solving their problems *for* them, I tried to *shepherd them* through their own problem-solving processes. My goal was to help them brainstorm alternatives, weigh the pros and cons of each potential solution in light of their own priorities and usher them towards making a well-thought-out decision that they felt was best for them. And keep in mind, you can offer your teen counsel, but don't be afraid of letting her fail if she chooses to ignore it.

Pain and Hurt Help You Grow

Whether my children fell down and skinned their knees as little tykes or experienced significant disappointments in their teenage years, my first instinct was to lessen their pain. While a band-aid and a kiss on a small knee go a long way toward fixing incidental boo-boos, young adult anguish is not so easily remedied.

Yet, I tried to impart the perspective that the contrast between good times and bad times sharpens our appreciation of life itself. During unexpectedly trying circumstances, that which we used to take for granted as "normal" takes on new significance. Adversity highlights the ordinary and mundane in a new and wonderful light. Hard times make us thankful for the routine and comfort of our everyday lives. We often don't realize how meaningful those "normal" things are until they are gone. By modeling an active appreciation for life with all its struggles and nurturing the discovery of beauty even when things are difficult, you can instill in your child the recognition that adversity forges a trail to her highest potential.

20

Set Adult Expectations Early On

Plant the Seeds When They are Young

Long before your child is actively hashing out what he intends to do after high school, set the stage by looking for opportunities to highlight good and bad examples that you observe around you. I can remember starting these casual conversations when my children were in fifth or sixth grade. As older friends or acquaintances made decisions that impacted their futures for better or for worse, I discussed those decisions and potential (or actual) outcomes with my children. Sometimes I asked them what they thought of a particular decision and how they might think through a similar scenario. Other times, I outlined how a young person's decision appeared either in alignment or out of alignment with the values of their family or our family.

The most common examples I highlighted involved options after completing high school. Through one of our common extracurricular activities, we encountered a young person whose parents had agreed to go into debt and spend a truckload of money on an out-of-state private university, even though many affordable, outstanding options were close to his home. I can remember telling my children it was hard to envision a scenario that involved our family being amenable to sinking that amount of money into college tuition. With numerous state colleges and universities available to us at a fraction of the cost, our family would likely see those choices as more closely aligned with our values of savings and stewardship. Even if it turned out it was possible to afford high-dollar tuition, it wouldn't be a probable event.

Over the span of their middle and high school years, I spoke with my children about viable, post-high school choices, emphasizing self-motivation as a key driver for maximizing future options. We discussed all manner of opportunities—full-time college, part-time college and part-time work, full-time work, trade school, apprenticeships, vocational careers and more. We talked frankly about college tuition ranges our family could afford, and I pointed out that they had the ever-existent prospect to work hard and excel academically, thereby increasing their pool of choices via fellowships or scholarships.

By bringing these topics up several years before my children faced the reality of them, I tried to ensure there were no surprises as they weighed their future choices. Understanding our family's reasonable expectations *up front* allowed my children to avoid pipe dreams and pursue their ambitious goals through well-informed decisions that were grounded in reality.

"Don't Be a Rainbow Basket Weaver"

"You can be a basket weaver if you want to be, but make sure you make all kinds and colors of baskets so you maximize your customer base. Don't just offer rainbow-colored baskets and then wonder why you can't support yourself. And if that is really your dream, I would suggest starting basket weaving as a hobby and initially building it as a side business. It might take some time to be profitable. In the meantime, figure out how you plan to maximize your chances of long-term employment, so that you can be financially independent and pursue your dream on a part-time basis until it is self-sustaining."

I used this amusing, far-fetched illustration throughout middle and high school to emphasize critical thinking in goal setting. I wanted my children to dream big and have unusual goals. At the same time, the pragmatic streak in me emphasized that a college education or trade school was not a fun-filled extension of high school. Given the cost of post-high school education, I wanted my children to think through major choices that would not only be enjoyable, but also provide them with a degree of job stability and lead to financial independence sooner, rather than later. Considering the significant monetary investment in tuition or job training, the goal was to actually emerge from college with a set of marketable skills and get a self-supporting job. With that broad qualification, the door remained wide open to pursue countless dreams and career opportunities. On countless occasions, I stressed to my children that by applying hard work, dedication, creativity and logic, they could aim high and reach for the skies.

Teach Them How to Work Toward Their Goals

Priority-setting can be *hard* for teenagers, especially if they are engaged in many activities that they love. In particular, I found my teens sometimes struggled with prioritizing daily and weekly activities in alignment with their long-terms goals. It was easy for them to get caught in the "here-and-now" and make a decision that might be more immediately gratifying, but ultimately hinder progress toward a medium-term or long-term desire.

The words "short-term, medium-term" and "long-term" are relative and often change depending on your age or perspective. For my teens, I estimated "short-term" goals as immediate to three months out. "Medium-term" goals were approximately three months to a year away. And "long-term" goals were generally classified as one to five years away. The *actual* time frames were not as important as the *action* of setting approximate time frames. With a mutually agreed-upon definition for "short-term, medium-term" and "long-term" goals, you can then take the next step in helping your teen categorize his ambitions into a priority framework.

In our family, we used a simple "tier system" to help our teens learn the discipline of prioritizing activities and time according to their long-term goals. During high school, their desired long-term goals centered around college and career choices.

"Tier One" included academics and advanced foreign language studies. My teens were interested in highly competitive universities that placed a premium on advanced foreign language studies. After being accepted to their target schools, my teens learned only a handful of incoming freshmen in their respective class years had achieved the same level of foreign language work they had prior to being accepted. Thus, their critical foreign language skills rendered a differentiating, distinct competitive edge over other applicants.

"Tier Two" included part-time jobs and extracurricular activities that were of special interest to the universities my teens had targeted. For example, successfully holding down a part-time job throughout the school year while still managing to maintain high academic performance demonstrated a strong work ethic, efficient multitasking skills and the ability to focus and prioritize. Achieving the level of black belt in martial arts showed discipline, commitment, perseverance and a high degree of physical fitness.

"Tier Three" included all of my teens' other activities.

How did my teens use these tiers in a practical way? Whenever they had to choose between activities competing for the same time slots on their schedules, the question I posed was (for each alternative), "Is this a Tier One, Two or Three activity?" At times, my children probably grew weary of hearing this query. But it eventually became ingrained into their decision-making processes, which was the whole point of the "Tier" system—to help *them* learn to keep long-term goals in the forefront of their minds, even while making daily and weekly short-term decisions regarding time expenditure.

By the end of high school, my children had internalized the "Tier" process and periodically used it going forward as a prioritization protocol for college and important life decisions, too. They were now independently setting their own short, medium and long-term goals, although they sometimes sought out counsel. I remember smiling broadly when I was talking with my college students on the phone and heard *them* say, "I decided to do X instead of Y, because X is a Tier One activity and Y is a Tier Two activity."

"Yessss," I remember thinking. "They got the message!"

Gradually Transition from Parental Authority to Parental Coach

There is no magic age when your child "grows up" or is suddenly mature enough to independently and responsibly manage his own life. One child may be ready as young as sixteen; for others, this type of maturity may not be apparent until sometime in their late twenties.

I draw an important distinction between "independence" and "responsible independence." A young adult can be financially self-supporting and making independent decisions that are not wise, mature or responsible. While this is indeed "independence," I do not define it as "responsible independence."

My aim was to dovetail my teens' "independence-readiness" and "mature responsibility" trajectories. Ideally, the development of their ability to be independent would merge smoothly with their increasing maturity. I knew if I could guide them through the process of interlocking "independence" and "responsibility," they would be well-positioned to make wise, thoughtful decisions for their own lives.

Watch your child as he grows through the teen years. Provide reasonable opportunities for him to test his readiness in making logical, independent decisions. Stand by to guide him if needed. The home environment is a safe place to experiment with independent decision-making, free from the pressure of irreversible long-lasting consequences if the decision is made poorly. I thought of my teen's high school years as an incubation period in which they could increasingly apply their blossoming decision-making skills.

How will you know if your teen is ready to begin making important decisions for himself? I looked for key indicators—"green lights," if you will—to ascertain when each of my children was prepared to sprout their decision-making wings. These guideposts gave me confidence that my children were marching in the right direction towards decision-making readiness. When I saw increasing demonstration of these attitudes, I knew it was time for me to continue morphing from "authority" to "coach." These guideposts gave me confidence that my children were marching in the right direction towards decision-making readiness:

- A humble recognition they were not yet "fully grown up" and still had much to learn about life;
- The willingness and desire to listen to and learn from a parent's life experiences with an open mind;
- Sound, logical thought processes that did not become overly clouded by emotions;
- Rational and practical prioritization of their activities;
- Keeping commitments and performing well in school, work, extracurriculars and home life;
- A respectfulness for parents, siblings and other family members that manifested itself in considerate words and actions.

Likewise, I consider the opposite of these characteristics as "red flags," indicating a *lack* of readiness to make responsible decisions. If you see red flags along the way, don't panic. Just take a step or two backwards in the "coaching" process and step a little deeper into "authority" role if need be. If you need to do this, explain the shift to your child so he understands it. Emphasize that you are on his side. Just like he wants to make his own wise decisions, *you* want that for him. Explain the readiness factors and attitudes you correlate with maturity. Express your concerns in an objective, non-threatening manner. Above all, when you see your teen accepting and understanding that you share the common goal of his independence, you can rest easy and know that you are on the right track.

21

Encouraging Versus Pushing

Teaching your young adult responsible independence is akin to teaching a bird to fly. *Encouraging* her out of the nest so that flying becomes *her* idea is more desirable than *pushing* her out of the nest when she doesn't want to fly. And encouraging her out of the nest is certainly more effective than ignoring the fact that she needs to learn to fly on her own. Ignoring flying lessons may result in your teen waking up one morning and shouting, "It's TIME!" as she recklessly leaps from the nest before her fledgling wings function properly. If she does that, you may have a mess to clean up.

It's Time for Them to Care "More" Than You Do

I learned the hard way blunt communication usually works better with teens than long, flowery explanations they tune out after the first two sentences. And so, my key messages to my children, especially in their eleventh and twelfth grade years, focused on brevity and directness. Basically, I became my mom.

"If by the end of eleventh grade, you don't care more about your future than I do, then I have done something wrong."

I remember the surprised look on my teens' faces the first time I declared this to each of them. I followed up with the simple explanation,

"You have had the privilege of a great education and loving, supportive parents. We have done our best to teach you what is most important in life and how to work towards your goals. If you are not motivated enough by now to pursue opportunities to build your own future, there isn't much I can do about that."

Understandably, some young adults may simply lack maturity in the latter high school years. That void can create the appearance of them "not caring" or being "unmotivated," when in actuality they are simply immature. If that had been the case with my children, I would have seriously suggested that they consider working full-time for a year or enlisting in the military for a stint to give themselves maturation time before pursuing next steps. I have known many young adults who did just that, and they emerged on the other side of those experiences with a high degree of clarity, focus and maturity. They had also acquired beneficial work experience, expert technical training and new life experiences that propelled them toward new, exciting paths.

Frequent Priority Reminders

As your teen peeks over the edge of the nest, she may get distracted with shiny pennies on the ground and forget that *flying* is the goal.

Learning to make short-term decisions that support long-term goals takes a lot of practice and reinforcement. It is much more fun to watch a movie than it is to study for that upcoming exam that could make or break your final grade. Going camping or hanging out with friends over the weekend can be infinitely more alluring than working ten-hour shifts at the grocery store.

Repetitively and gently remind your teen of her priority "tiers." Help her see that proper prioritization and effective time management often translates into time for her to do all —or most—of the fun things she wishes to do. It just might mean she enjoys those activities via delayed gratification instead of instantaneous gratification. You might feel like a broken record as you redundantly question, "Is it Tier One, Two or Three?" That's okay. Your job is to shake your teen out of unnecessary distraction. Your repetitive inquiry will help her glance up from the shiny pennies and refocus on her real goals.

Ask Questions That Make Them Think

In Chapter Two, I listed a series of questions to ask *yourself* as you framed your parenting goals. As you move from parenting authority to parenting coach, it is time to rephrase these questions into an ongoing self-reflective tool for your *teen*. These questions are not meant to be asked all at once (Heavens! That would be overwhelming for a full-grown adult!). Nor do they need to be answered aloud. Think of them as casual rhetorical questions that you pose when the time seems right.

- What kind of a person do you want to be? List three positive characteristics that you would like to pop into other people's minds when they think of you.
- What are your most important personal and family moral values? Try to pick no less than three and no more than ten. Prioritize them in rank order.
- How do you want to treat and interact with other people—those you know and those you don't know? How about those you agree with and those you disagree with? How can you mesh your desired character attributes with your interpersonal relationships?
- What kind of education or job training do you aspire to?
- What kind of job do you want? Will that support the type of lifestyle you hope to enjoy? Will it allow you to independently support yourself throughout life and save for your future needs?
- Consider your strengths and weaknesses. What do you need to change within yourself to become the best person you can be? Set three personal improvement goals with target achievement dates for yourself. After you have achieved (or made significant progress towards) those, set three more goals. Repeat.

Minimize Idle Time and Maximize Productive Pursuits

People have asked me, "how did you keep your teens out of trouble?" Aside from the many principles I've previously outlined, my answer to that is keep them *busy*. If you want to raise a responsible teen and foster her zest for life, keep her busy and having fun with wholesome, challenging extracurricular activities led by responsible adults. If you live in an area where there is not a large selection of organized extracurriculars, creatively brainstorm ideas with your teen. Think about pursuits that could teach her leadership, a strong work ethic, a spirit of volunteerism, generosity to others, physical fitness or competitiveness. Figure out together how your teen can spearhead a new program in your area. Encourage your young adult to stretch beyond her comfort zone and develop new competencies. Help her to recognize that she can *create* opportunities for herself if she can't find existing ones. Geography doesn't need to be an obstacle to your teen's productive pursuits if you and she resolve that you will successfully find or invent "out-of-the-box" options. As my mom used to say, "Where there's a will, there's a way."

Encourage Them to Think of Others More Than Themselves

As my teenagers approached the end of their high school years, I wanted them to think, "What can I do for others in the world around me?" more often than "What can others in the world do for me?" To me, this shift from self-orientation to others-orientation, represents a distinguishing hallmark of mature adult perception.

To be sure, there are many decisions young adults need to make that are naturally centered around themselves—"Should I go to college? If so, where? What do I want to study? What career do I want? Where will I live? How will I support myself?"

This kind of "self-focus" is different from being "selfishly-focused." Self-focus is necessary as your young adult plans the detailed direction of her life. It ebbs and flows during times of urgent or time-sensitive planning like choosing a college, buying a car or finding an apartment.

A young adult can be self-focused in areas that demand her immediate attention, but still be considerate and attentive to other people. On the other hand, a selfishly-focused teen thinks about her own needs and ignores those of other people. If you notice your teen developing a habit of being inconsiderate to others, nip it in the bud. Gently point out specific examples of inconsideration to her and ask her how she could have handled those situations in a more thoughtful way.

Self-Initiated Consideration Goes Both Ways

I wanted my teens to develop the quality of self-initiated consideration in their words and actions towards parents, each other, other family members, friends and people they met out in the world as they grew into their expanding lives. It is one thing to train and instruct young children to be kind and considerate. You can model this type of behavior from the beginning and reinforce it throughout the childhood years. However, at some point, my hope was that my young adults would show consideration towards others because they *wanted* to, not because they *had* to.

One of the ways you can encourage the ongoing development of this attribute in your young adult after she has left home is by giving *her* similar consideration. If she is managing her responsibilities well, not getting into trouble and working hard, treat her like an adult, not like a high schooler. Don't be a clingy parent and place unreasonable expectations on her that you wouldn't place on another adult.

I remember an acquaintance of mine once told me she was not satisfied with the frequency of her college student's phone calls home. She shared that her son's academic performance was stellar, he was involved in several exciting extracurricular clubs and attended church each week. He even texted her several times each week. Yet she remained frustrated he did not *call* home every week.

She mentioned she and her husband had recently informed their son that he "must" call home once a week. While I agreed a minimal once-a-week phone call would be nice, I was rather aghast that they had stipulated this as a "requirement" for their responsibly independent son. To me, that type of demand seemed controlling and unhealthy. Furthermore, it seemed like the quickest way to guarantee the exact *opposite* of what the parents wished for over the long term—consistent, loving communication with their son.

If you find yourself in an analogous situation with your mature young adult, I suggest you first stop and ask yourself how *you* would want to be treated by another adult. Then, act accordingly toward *your* young adult. Be careful that you don't inadvertently cause a boomerang effect with oppressive restrictions that you can't really enforce and that appear manipulative to your young adult. Blowing that kind of hot air may come back to bite you in the rear end. Instead of getting a happy, upbeat phone call once every two weeks and chatty texts in between calls, you may wind up with no communication at all.

22

Young Adults...Yikes! What Now?

Compete Against Yourself

Ideally, as your teen nears the end of high school, he accepts that in many of his endeavors, there will be people who will outshine him. Likewise, he humbly recognizes that he will sometimes outshine others.

Your responsibly independent young adult will have reflected on his own strengths and weaknesses throughout the previous few years. He now understands self-improvement is an ongoing process throughout life and with strong resolve, he can set goals and achieve them. With a healthy view of his competencies, he is poised to enter adulthood, realizing his ultimate competitor is himself. While he may actively compete against other individuals or groups for external rewards in academic performance, athletics, the fine arts or employment opportunities, his intrinsic motivation stems from a strong desire to do his best and stretch his fabric.

Demonstrate a Strong Work Ethic in All You Do

A complete work ethic is comprised of inner attitude and outward demonstration. In other words, my attitude about my tasks plus how I perform my tasks equals my total work ethic. I tried to help my young adults learn that although the two components may seem at odds with each other, you can still make progress toward improving your overall work ethic.

Occasionally, my teens would express the sentiment, "But I don't *feel* like doing it," concerning a perceived less-than-desirable task. My mom once again occupied my mouth and I would hear my own voice saying, "There are many things adults *have* to do but may not always *want* to do. Being responsible means remaining committed to the job. Whatever you do, whether it is something you want to do or not, do it with excellence, so that you don't let *yourself* down."

I can remember discussing the cliché, "Fake it till you make it," with my teens, to reference how repetitiously completing undesirable tasks with demonstrable excellence and a positive outward attitude could eventually *transform* internal complaining into internal enthusiasm. I explained that although this might not happen with every unenjoyable task they encountered, it would go a long way towards helping them objectively see what they could gain from experiences they did not relish.

Rejoice in Other People's Accomplishments

I took a swig from my now-warm water bottle and adjusted my damp sun visor. It had been a sweltering day to stand in the shade, much less tear around on a tennis court like my son had done since sunrise. I glanced across the venue, watching him pack up his red and white gear bag, which was almost as big as his younger sister. His clothes clung to him like he had hopped into a swimming pool fully dressed. As he walked over to his opponent to say a final farewell, I could tell from the look on his face that disappointment overruled exhaustion at the moment. After winning several rounds earlier in the day, my son had advanced to this match—the semi-final for his age bracket. The winner would earn the right to play in the coveted final tomorrow.

The semi-final did not go well. My son had played his hardest—and he had played well. His opponent had simply played better than he had today.

I saw my son force a cheerful smile and his words of congratulations wafted across the court. Their match had been one of the last ones of the day and the arena, which had been a beehive of activity earlier in the afternoon, had ceased its buzzing frenzy of players, coaches, referees, parents and other assorted fans.

The victor stood up, shook my son's hand and gave him a sweaty "bro-hug." I couldn't hear what he said, but the impact of his words coaxed a big grin onto my son's face. He loped off the court and headed towards me.

The previous week, I had watched my daughter cheer for her gymnastics teammates as they competed in the last qualifying meet leading up to the State Championships in one month. Her heart and spirit were doing back handsprings down the floor exercise mat, but unfortunately her broken ankle prevented her body from cooperating. After a season of great meet performances and high hopes of placing well in the all-around State competition, my daughter was sidelined with a big black boot adorning her left ankle. She still attended practices, laboring through repetitive sets of strength work designed to keep her in shape as much as possible. She was excited for her teammates, but I knew the bitter pill of disappointment had been hard to swallow when she landed askew on her tumbling run a couple of weeks earlier. The moment she had landed, she had known her ankle was broken. And as her coach helped her up, supporting her so she could hop off the mat on the other foot, I knew that picking up the pieces of her heart was not going to be quite as easy.

Disappointments and failures taught my children to rejoice in the successes of their friends and their adversaries. When they were younger, they had learned intellectually that being happy for others' achievements was a character attribute our family valued. However, learning from hearing about it is quite different than learning from experiencing it. The latter requires a lot more fortitude.

I used disappointing experiences like these to reinforce with my children that personal setbacks do not erase the potential for new and future opportunities. I pointed out that even if they were vying for one slot and they lost that particular chance, many other related possibilities exist in this world. If other exciting opportunities aren't readily apparent, you might just have to search a little longer and work a lot harder to find them – or create them.

I tried to impress on my teens that allowing yourself to dwell in resentment, envy or jealousy of other people carries with it the opportunity cost of diminishing *your* creative, productive energy. Instead of making you feel better, I explained, envy leaves you depleted and feeling sorry for yourself. I told them I had found that when I stopped feeling sorry for myself after disappointing experiences, worked hard at feeling genuinely happy for my competitor's victory and recalled the many things I was thankful for, disappointment eventually fell into its proper place. Looking back after some time had passed, it was easier to have greater clarity and perspective. Then I could see what lessons I learned from failure and use that wisdom going forward.

These hard-fought disappointments were tangible eye-openers in my teens' lives. I told them when I had experienced failure in my life, one of the ways I had dealt with it was to allow myself a day or two to be really sad about it. But by day three, I pulled myself out of the mucky slough of despond and back into the hopeful land of planning my next steps.

Basic Life Skills

Many resources offer long lists of life skills to teach your high school students before they leave home, so I won't try to recreate the wheel here.

As "life events" occurred in our family, (selling or buying a home, switching insurance companies, selling or buying a car, handling fraudulent credit card charges, etc.), we communicated how these things worked to our children in a way they could understand, according to their ages. Our ongoing messages to our preteens and teens throughout middle school and high school focused on our family's view of financial management. These topics and perspectives included:

Saving & Investments–

Develop a habit of regular and disciplined savings, even if the amount you are saving is small at first. Take advantage of the compounding effect of money by initiating retirement savings as soon as you get your first job.

Tithing/Charitable Giving–

Set aside a certain percentage of money from every paycheck as a tithe for your faith or for charitable giving. Aim for ten percent. You will be surprised at what will happen to your finances over your lifetime if you prioritize tithing and giving.

Budgeting–

Know how much money you are earning and keep track of how much you are spending, as well as what you are spending it on. We made sure our teens understood that budgets don't "work" or "not work" by themselves; ultimately you *make* a budget "work" by sticking to it. If you ignore it, it "won't work" for you.

Credit Cards–

If you exercise self-control, credit cards are a safe and more convenient way to purchase than using cash or debit card. Don't spend more than you are able to pay off *completely* at the end of every statement period.

Self-Sufficiency–

Be excited about being self-sufficient and financially responsible for yourself. It may take a lot of hard work, but it marks the beginning of full independence/adulthood.

Housing–

Choose a housing option you can afford, given your other expenses and financial commitments. Set a budget threshold and don't exceed it, whether you are renting or purchasing. If you take out a loan to purchase a home, do not max out the amount of loan you can get. Make sure that you are comfortable with your monthly payments, not biting your nails each month wondering if you have enough to pay your bills.

Automobiles–

Avoid buying brand-new cars. They depreciate significantly the moment you drive them out of the dealer's parking lot, and you don't recoup that money. Instead, look for a reliable, well-kept vehicle with low mileage for its age. Identify your other key criteria, and decide on your budget. When you purchase your car, take good care of it. Be diligent with its routine maintenance so that it lasts as long as possible. Drive it until it dies.

Insurance–

Whether you are contemplating auto, homeowner's, renter's or life insurance, do your homework. Get a few estimates, so that you can identify if one seems inordinately expensive. Throughout the years, periodically check different companies to see if you can find better rates for the same coverage.

Teach Them Accountability for Their Own Happiness

As my teens prepared to enter the adult world, discussions regarding accountability for their own emotions and happiness became more frequent. Their blossoming life experiences provided interesting fodder for periodic discussions on sticky topics. These weren't planned monologues or debates. I timed my messages carefully and considerately, unless the urgency of an issue demanded immediate discussion. I usually began with a preamble such as, "You might not want to hear what I have to say, but I would much rather you hear it from me first than from your boss, coach, teacher or friend. Dialogue starters included:

- People won't always be nice to you.
- People won't always care what you think.
- People won't always let you "have your say".
- In terms of what you say and do in response to these people, it is still best to take the "high road".
- Other people cannot "make" you feel a certain way. Other people or circumstances cannot "make or break" your happiness. Other people may say mean or even abusive things to you. They may also treat you unkindly or unfairly. As an adult, you can *choose* to allow their words and actions to control the way you think about yourself, or you can recognize their issues for exactly what they are—*their issues*. You don't have to believe anything they say or do has a connection to you at all. When someone loses their temper and lashes out at you, it is *their* problem, not yours.
- Take full responsibility for your own feelings. If you believe other people control your emotions, you abdicate your mental fortitude and make yourself a victim. If you want to be happy, you can *choose* to be happy. If you want to be sad and gloomy, you can *choose* to be sad and gloomy. You can find joy in the present, even if you wish things were different. But don't fool yourself into thinking that your emotions are controlled by other people

or circumstances. They are controlled by *you* and what you allow yourself to *think*.

- Focus on the good, positive things in life. Surround yourself with people who are positive and uplifting, not with people who drag you down. If you find yourself dwelling on perceived negatives, identify and create more positives around you. You can always find something beautiful in each day, even if it comes in the form of a tiny wildflower, the soulful sound of a train rumbling by or the steady pattering of a drenching rain.
- Do not believe the "grass is always greener" on the other side. If you let the discontentment "vacuum" roar in your brain, it will suck the joy out of your life.
- Training yourself to be fully responsible for your own thoughts and feelings is an ongoing and challenging process. It takes an incredible amount of discipline, character strength and determination. Most adults have not mastered it.

In the end, I hoped that I could give my young adults a jumpstart in learning accountability for their own emotions sooner, rather than later. Looking back on my life, that was a lesson I didn't fully grasp until well into adulthood. I believed if they understood these concepts, they would be better prepared from the start to succeed in making their dreams a reality.

Epilogue

How Do You Know if Your Parenting Was Successful?

I reached across the kitchen counter for my buzzing phone. I was chopping vegetables for a healthy curry when my daughter called. She was six weeks away from finishing her undergraduate degree and had been submerged in online apartment hunting in the city where she would be attending graduate school. Apparently, she had surfaced for air.

Although she was living across the county and unable to see potential apartments in person, her older brother currently lived in the city she was headed to and had visited her "final two". He was also about to relocate to another city and had just locked in his new living quarters.

"Hi there!"

"Hi, Mom! Mom, I'm about to sign the lease on my apartment! I've read it all carefully and everything seems to be in order. But I wanted to read it to you just in case there's something I'm missing. Do you have a few minutes?"

"Of course."

Cradling the phone between my shoulder and ear, I set my chopping aside and washed my hands. I wanted to concentrate fully as my daughter read the lease.

A few minutes and a couple of questions later, we said goodbye, sufficiently confident that all was well.

I smiled as I resumed chopping. This daughter—the one who had corresponded with numerous real estate agents and landlords...the one who had navigated the apartment application process...the one who had researched and negotiated special terms into her lease...this daughter was the same young woman who had been very concerned four years earlier when she left home for college that she would not be ready to do "adult" things when she graduated. This young woman, who was now embarking on a graduate degree in a math and science-related field, was the same one who didn't like math in high school. And this competent young adult who had sought my ear as a double-check sounding board was the same person who used to take offense if I offered an opinion about something she already knew.

And my son. This son—the one who had carved out time to visit apartments for his sister during arguably one of his busiest weeks in the past two years of graduate school...the one whose thesis due date was looming near...the one who was busily writing and simultaneously coordinating a cross-country move ...this son was the same young man whose idea of time management in high school resembled, quite often, a hot mess. This young man, who was now about to complete graduate school and embark on his professional career, was the same one who had flown out the door to get to tennis practice on time in ninth grade, only to discover after the thirty-minute ride that he had forgotten to put on his tennis shoes when he left the house. And this loving brother was the same person who had abjectly refused to share his toys with his sister at age six.

These two strong, independently-minded adults, who are now the best of friends, were the same children who drove me nuts arguing with each other many times a day from ages seven to eleven. Their arguments were my alarm clock for a long time. One morning, I woke up to silence. It was eerie. I bolted out of bed, ran to the family room and found them...playing happily together.

I added the remainder of the now-chopped vegetables to the pot and stirred in some seasonings.

It seemed to me that the apartment adventure encapsulated the entirety of our parenting journey in a brush stroke. All of the time and all of the effort we invested now illustrated a cohesive picture.

As the delicious aroma of the bubbling curry permeated the house, so too the outcome of resolved parenting now spread throughout our family relationships. From the beginning, I wanted our home to be a haven—a refuge from the craziness of the world—where peace, love and acceptance abounded. Although our children no longer live in our home, they have absorbed that goal and made it their own. Their current relationships with each other and with their parents are evidence that parenting from a place of principle, perseverance and determination was worth it. They are thriving, successful and responsibly-independent adults.

You can "measure" parenting success both objectively and subjectively. The objective instrument of character report cards I previously outlined in detail created a track record that showed my children's progress in our family's pre-determined character attributes over the years. Looking back at their character grades is like a walk down memory lane. I can see and remember the areas where each child struggled and eventually succeeded. I suppose if I wanted to, I could actually graph their character development progress. I never did, but I had the data to do so.

In recent years, I can see more clearly than ever that our parenting was successful because of the way our adult children now *live their lives*. Subjectively, I wonder and ponder how all of the parenting puzzle pieces interlocked over time. Sometimes when I was in the midst of parenting, it seemed very complex. But now, with the benefit of many years of reflection and hindsight, I see that the basic principles are pretty simple.

When you need an energy or confidence boost, remind yourself you want your child to turn out to be a great young adult. Parenting is about raising a *human being* and inculcating values that will help her succeed at whatever productive path she chooses in life. Take a deep breath, roll up your sleeves, buckle down and put in the "grunt work" of parenting. Bringing a cute, little, cuddly baby home from the hospital was the easy part. That part went by very quickly, just like the puppy stage for a dog or kitten stage for a cat. Then you are left with an adventurous imp of a toddler and a growing child who explores and tests everything under the sun. Appreciate the beauty of your little human being. Marvel in her discoveries. Love her like crazy. Teach her well. Parent her like you mean it.

Afterword

When I began jotting down notes about parenting to document my thoughts for my children, I never dreamed my scribbles would morph into a personal mission to help other parents.

This book started out as a series of random ideas, written on scrap paper, napkins, paper towels and whatever else I could find to write on when a thought struck.

Raising a child and writing a book are studies of contrasts and comparisons, but they are more alike than different. Parenting was "pedal to the metal" from start to finish, writing this book has likewise been a tumultuous journey. Raising my children required me to work to improve myself as a person; writing this book has also refined who I am. When I became a parent, I was not confident in my ability to successfully raise human beings; when I began writing this book, I was not confident in my ability to complete it. Raising my children required significant strategy, time and energy; explaining *how* I parented in these pages required extensive thought, planning and writing. In both parenting and writing, I learned that my *dreams* had to become *disciplines* in order to be fruitful.

My parenting wasn't perfect, nor is this book. With both endeavors, I gave my best, just as I taught my children to do. I hope and pray you might find my thoughts beneficial in some way for your family as you parent like you mean it.

Acknowledgements

I was blessed with four devoted parents, each of whom served as a shining example. I must start by thanking them all for the foundation and influence they provided not only for me, but also for my children.

Dad and Mom One, you weren't here on Earth during my parenting journey, but not an event occurred in the lives of my children when I didn't imagine what you would do or say had you been here. Your love, devotion, faith and confidence in me shaped my life and the lives of the grandchildren you never met. Your unexpected departure planted the seed in my mind to write this book. There are so many questions I didn't have a chance to ask you about parenting. And since none of us knows which day will be our last, I wanted to pass on to my adult children my recollections of your wisdom as well as my own experiences and learning as I raised them. That way, if they become parents someday and I'm not here, at least they might find some questions answered. I also hope that somehow, our shared parenting principles might benefit and inspire other families.

Dad and Mom Two, I could not have been more thrilled when you announced that you were moving to be close to us, when our children were infant and toddler ages. Your love, support, prayers and guidance throughout the years have been invaluable. Thank you for loving and raising your own wonderful sons in such a way as to provide parenting inspiration for me. Thank you for uplifting me on those challenging days when I was convinced I was doing something terribly wrong as a mother. Your reminder of, "Line upon line, precept upon precept," gave me the determination to persevere in spite of myself. Your listening ears always offered me a safe place to share my thoughts and excitement, ask questions, and sometimes, vent my frustrations. Thank you for not only being my yoga buddies, but also nonjudgmental spiritual encouragers. Thank you for laughing with me. And thank you for being such an integral part of our family's and children's lives in more ways than I can possibly enumerate. Your loving, joyful investment in our children's lives is a priceless gift. I know that my own parents were also incredibly grateful for you.

Ray and Lori Collins, your expertise on our state education requirements and timely suggestions over the course of more than a decade helped me navigate the legalities and administrative side of our children's homeschooling education program. Thank you for going above and beyond in your roles at Allendale Academy to support our children's dreams.

Valerie Clark, your professional editing improved my work and enhanced the strength of my message. Thank you for encouraging me and generously sharing your overall publishing expertise.

To my children—you constantly amaze and inspire me. Thank you for cheering me on and believing I could write this book. It was a privilege and honor to raise you. I am so thankful you are our children.

To my husband Phil—I will honor your request not to be embarrassed in writing. But you know.

Resources

About Allendale Academy

Allendale Academy is a K-12 virtual umbrella school for home-schooled students and is registered as a private school with the Florida Department of Education. Additionally, Allendale is registered with the College Board, the National Collegiate Athletic Association (NCAA), National Association of Intercollegiate Athletics (NAIA), Bright Futures, Florida Virtual School (FLVS) and the Florida Parent-Educators Association (FPEA). It is a private school dedicated and equipped to assist parents nationwide in educating their children in the most supportive environment, the home.

When you enroll your child in Allendale Academy, you accept the responsibilities and duties of being your child's teacher in your home. Allendale provides the registration and documentation (report cards, attendance forms and transcripts) to satisfy most states' requirements for private education. Upon request, Allendale can also provide guidelines for scope and sequence, as well as suggestions concerning available curricula.

Since its founding in 1985 through the end of the 2021 school year, Allendale Academy has graduated over 2,000 students. Allendale graduates have received Florida's Bright Futures Scholarships, the José Martí Scholarship, NCAA scholarships and, in 2013, one young lady received the prestigious Gates Millennium Scholarship. Allendale alumni have been admitted to major universities, all four of the United States military service academies, serve in the military and as first responders, and have pursued every career imaginable.

About the Author

D. I. Clark has a special passion for helping adults and children feel competent, courageous and confident in their daily lives.

She has taught and coached parents and children of all ages for nearly 40 years. She holds an undergraduate degree in Communications, as well as an MBA. She has tutored both locally and internationally. Prior to raising and educating her children, she held positions in broadcasting, higher education and corporate finance.

In her free time, she enjoys spending time with her family, biking, hiking, martial arts, yoga and gardening.

CPSIA information can be obtained
at www.ICGtesting.com
Printed in the USA
LVHW031157040222
710173LV00001B/27